Romantic Essex

First Edition	.	.	.	*April*	1901
Second Edition	.	.	.	*July*	1907
This Edition	.	.	.	*November*	2001

Originally published by J. M. Dent MDCCCCI. Reprinted MDCCCCVII. This edition reset in Baskerville and printed MMI.
Photography, Typesetting, Design & Reproduction © 2001 by PBK Publishing. Doddinghurst, Essex. (01277 822913)
All reasonable effort has been made to contact the copyright holder within the terms of the Copyright Act
Anyone claiming copyright should contact the Publisher.

ISBN 0-9536634-2-6

Printed by The Lavenham Press Ltd, Water St, Lavenham, Sudbury, Suffolk

To

Kitty and Maurice

CAMBRIDGESHIRE

ROYSTON

HERTFORD

SHIRE

LONDON

KENT

0° E   30'

52°
N

30'

Hadstock   Bartlow
Gt Chesterford   Sturmer   R. S
Elmdon   Strethall   5   Ashdon   R. Colne
                  Littlebury   Stambourne
                  SAFFRON   Castle
                  WALDEN   25
Newport   Lit. Sampford   Finchingfield
            Thaxted   Wethers-
4   field
Henham   Tiltey   Bardfield
Elsenham   14   Bocking   Bla
            Gt. Easton   Braintree   Cres
        Dunmow   Chelmer   Lit. Dunmow
        Gt.   Felstead
Hallingbury   Li   Gt. Canfield   Lit Leighs
            Hatfield   Pleshey   Gt.   Fai
23   Broad Oak   High Easter   Leighs   Chipp
        THE   Mash-   Gt. Waltham   WITH
        Harlow RODINGS   bury   15   Hatfield
        Netteswell   Willingale   Broomfield
Broxbourne   Roydon   Chignall   New Hall
        Potter   Springfie
Nazing   Street   Fyfield   CHELMSFORD   MA
        Epping   Ongar   Gt. Baddow   Do
Waltham   Sandon
Abbey   Greenstead   Blackmore   Galleywood   Pur
20   Theydon   21   Fry-   Margaretting Stow
Loughton   Roding   Dodding   erning   ngatestone   Hullbridge
        Havering   hurst   Shenfield   Mountnessing
Chingford   atte-Bower   Sth   Brent-   Billericay   Bat
Woodford   R.   Weald   wood   Lit   Gt   bri
        Wanstead Park   22   Burstead   Hac
            E. Horndon   Thundersley   Ray
        R. Lea   Laindon   Pitsea   Ha
    Barking   S. Ben fleet
East Ham   Rainham   S. Ockendon   Bulphan   19   Canve
        Avely   Orsett
        Purfleet   Stifford   RIVER THA
            Chadwell

0°   East of Greenwich   30'

Map: Peter Kurton

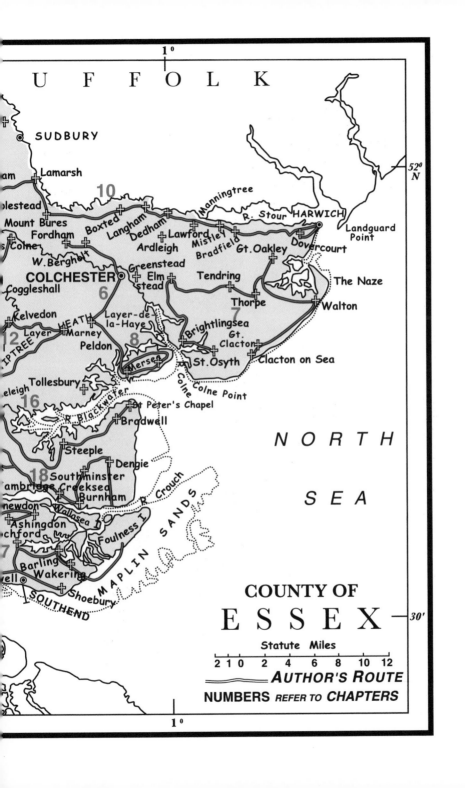

S U F F O L K

1°

52°
N

SUDBURY

am Lamarsh

10

Manningtree

olestead

Mount Bures Boxted Langham Dedham

R. Stour HARWICH

Landguard
Point

Fordham

Lawford Mistley

s Colne

Ardleigh Bradfield Gt. Oakley

Dovercourt

W. Berghost

COLCHESTER

Greenstead

Elm

stead

Tendring

The Naze

Coggleshall

6

Thorpe

Walton

Kelvedon

Layer-de-

HEATH la-Haye

7

12

Layer Marney

Peldon

8

Brightlingsea

Gt.

Clacton

Clacton on Sea

PTREE

eleigh Tollesbury

16

R. Blackwater

Mersea

St. Osyth

Colne Point

Colne

St Peter's Chapel

Bradwell

Steeple

Dengie

18

Southminster

ambridge Creeksea

newdon Wallasea I.

Burnham

R. Crouch

M A P L I N   S A N D S

Ashingdon

chford

7

Foulness I.

Barling

ell Wakering

SOUTHEND

Shoebury

N O R T H

S E A

COUNTY OF

E S S E X

30'

Statute Miles

2 1 0   2   4   6   8   10 12

AUTHOR'S ROUTE

NUMBERS REFER TO CHAPTERS

Romantic Essex
Pedestrian Impressions

By

Reginald A. Beckett

" The addition of strangeness to beauty constitutes
the romantic." — W. Pater.

PBK Publishing
Doddinghurst
Essex
MMI

Prefatory Note to the Second Edition

IN issuing a cheaper edition of this little book, I have to express my thanks to the publishers, who have taken some pains to discover my present place of exile in order to repeat their first risky venture ; to the critics, who were almost invariably courteous, and in most cases remarkably kind ; to numerous correspondents, some who have been good enough to offer valuable notes and suggestions ; and to the book-reading public, who, in their readiness to recognise an honest labour of love, were not deterred by an unpromising subject or the amateur craftsmanship of an unknown writer.

A few necessary corrections in points of detail have now been made. Further improvements would involve rewriting the book, for which leisure is lacking. In response to several requests, an itinerary map has been added.

The *Green Man* at Finchingfield was unfortunately burnt down early in 1905. I am consoled by thinking that the old house is saved from possible future profanation. A picture of it as it appeared when I stayed there is given as a frontispiece.

R. A. B

BUDAPEST
January 1907

Preface to this edition

Too valuable a work to be left unappreciated and forgotten on a dusty second hand bookshop shelf, this minor masterpiece has now been rescued for posterity and is republished after one hundred years.

To judge by the wide scope of his subject matter it is clear that the author spent a great deal of time exploring the county's highways and byways, noting villages castles farmsteads churches and towns.

During an era when everything was changing he shunned even the humble bicycle, preferring to travel on foot absorbing the essence of Essex in the twilight of the Victorian age

He rested overnight at the inns, which abounded in the county, where a warm welcome could always be found.

His observation of the people he met along the way is truly wonderful, full as it is of genuine appreciation and subtle humour.

Some of the elderly people he encountered during the late nineteenth century would have been children during the Napoleonic Wars. They themselves had mixed with people of an even earlier age. We can almost reach out and touch them.

It is hoped that the more adventurous reader may wish to retrace some of the author's steps, so the original map has been redrawn at a larger size, and to accompany it photographs are included of some of the locations as they are now.

Here then is a bridge to the past and to another age.

Doddinghurst

November 2001

Ed

xii

Contents

xiii

Illustrations

Romantic Essex

I

An Undiscovered Country

" The charming, friendly English landscape ! Is there any in
the world like it ? "– *Thackeray*.

IN this age of travel, the word " undiscovered "
can never be used except in a relative sense. The
Balkan States are becoming hackneyed, the jealously-guarded secrets of Thibet arouse but a faint
curiosity, and lion-hunting in Central Africa forms
part of the advertised programme of a personally-
conducted tour. The spirit of exploration to-day,
like that of military glory in the past, sighs for
more worlds to conquer. The only remedy seems
to be — as in contemporary food problems — a
system of intensive culture. We must seek out
the mystery that underlies the obvious. Turning
back upon our steps, we find a well-spring of
romance at home. Hence it has been suggested
by Mr Alfred Rimmer that some tourist agency
should organise excursions into Middlesex. But
whether in Middlesex or Morocco, the seeing eye
is the main thing. " What do you call this place ? "
said one tourist to another, in the hearing of Long-

fellow, on the steps of the hotel at Interlachen. " I have been here two hours already, and find it devilish dull."

The general ignorance of Essex is still astonishing. Here is a beautiful district lying at our very doors, which to the great majority of travellers from the metropolis, is a veritable unknown land. Yet the historic interest, at least, of a county situated so near to London and the Thames, and necessarily the theatre of many events that have helped to shape our destinies, must be obvious enough.

Nine people out of ten are struck with amazement when you speak of Essex as a holiday field. They imagine it as an utter abomination of desolation, It is an article of faith with many that there are no hills in Essex. With those who know better, this assertion only provokes a smile ; but, as happens with most vulgar errors, it dies hard. Like the primal curse pronounced upon man, it can only be expiated by the sweat of his brow. It is true that other parts of England can show bolder heights, lovelier rivers, more opulent architecture than Essex ; but for variety of interest, and for a certain homelike sweetness which excites not only admiration but affection, Essex bears the palm.

Let the reader look attentively at the outline of this slighted county on the map. He will see in the first place how beautifully the coast-line is broken up by tidal rivers and estuaries, by creeks and islands. Next, he will notice that along the coast near the sea and its inlets the country rises into irregular hills. This juxtaposition has all the elements of the picturesque. He will further observe that Essex is divided on the north from the rich lands of Suffolk by the river Stour, made famous by Constable, with its meadows and water-mills ; and on the west from Hertfordshire by the Stort and the Lea, the haunts of the Compleat Angler. Still studying the map he sees (what is indeed historically true) that the Epping Forest which Londoners know so well forms but a part of the great stretch of woodland which once covered nearly the whole of the county, and of which other indications survive in Hainault Forest, Hat-field Forest, and such names as Forest Gate, and North and South Weald. Though much of the forest has gone, the student will rightly conclude that the richly-wooded character of the country cannot wholly have disappeared. Looking farther north, in the corner of the county where Hertford-shire and Cambridge adjoin it, clusters of hills are observed which are common to all three counties, and are in reality chalk downs, being part of the same formation as those at Royston and Dunstable. As to the great central heart of the county, intersected by the main railway line, I am not sure but that this is most interesting of all. It is the great corn district, where, even to-day, after all the terrible agricultural depression, stretches acre after acre of the " tall Essex wheat " which was once so famous, traversed in all direct- tions by delightful shady lanes.   One may imagine what this country was like before the exigencies of commerce compelled us to fetch our food from abroad — when England grew her own corn ; and what a sturdy and prosperous peasantry these strong wheat lands must have maintained.   One can read the character of the old inhabitants in the houses that they built.   The true Essex cottage is of quite a distinct type, and is charac- teristic in its roomy homeliness and fitness for its purpose.   Another indication of former prosperity, and one at which travellers to-day have every reason to rejoice, is the general prevalence of good and comfortable, though quite unpretentious, inns; and it is noteworthy that this feature is absent only in those district, such as Tiptree Heath where the land was comparatively poor and un- productive.

But not only in its natural features, or in its cottages and inns, does the interest of Essex lie. Here, as elsewhere, in spite of all the well-inten- tioned efforts of churchwardens and " restoring " patrons, the Churches enshrine the relics of the glory of Gothic architecture.   The churches are for the most part small and homely in character, but none the less beautiful for that ; and still there remain here and there, for the reverence and delight of the understanding eye, miracles of simplicity and elegance, wrought in wood and stone, just as they left the hand of the mediæval craftsman. Mr Thomas Hardy, whose novels repay study for their knowledge of architecture alone, says in one of them that the conscious imitation of Gothic forms has gone so far in our day that it will be difficult for the student in the future to distinguish between the actual work of the builders of old times and the mere reproduction of that work by modern hands. I venture to think that there is one style to which this remark is less applicable than to others, namely, the Norman. Early in date, imperfect in development, often heavy and overloaded as it is, for these very reasons it is seldom copied or replaced; and thus the chance of fictitious Norman work being palmed off upon our descendants is but small. Essex is peculiarly rich in Norman remains; and as one stands in admiration before some richly-moulded round-headed arch or doorway, one thinks how it expresses the life and character of the people who built it, and what a long road that people has travelled since, eagerly pursuing its external aggrandisement, and turning its back upon these silent yet eloquent witnesses to its own past. Just as when along some quiet road we see above the trees the quaint chimneys and gables of a Tudor mansion, and, drawing nearer, perceive the gleam of water beyond the hedge, and judge from its shape and stillness, its swans and dreaming lilies,

6   An Undiscovered Country

that it was what we fancied — a moat; we reflect
on the time when this was to the house a
necessary means of isolation and defence.   The
very nomenclature of the county has its tale to
tell, beginning with unintelligible names that point
to a remote Celtic origin, followed by the Anglo-
Roman *Colchester* or *Chesterford*, with innumerable
Saxon names of pure descriptive charm, such as
Fairstead, Elmstead, Guestingthorpe, or *Bradfield* ;
after these come the double names indicative of
Norman predominance, such as *Layer de La Haye,
Norton Mandeville, Tolleshunt D'Arcy,* and many
others ;   while others again are quaintly provocative
of curiosity, as *Wimbish, Wendens Ambo,* or *Shellow
Bowells.*

Although the simple life of these villages is as
different as may be from the life of our large cities,
there is no district where one may feel more completely at home.   For one thing, the land has been
well settled and carefully tilled, at least in the past,
and is so thickly sprinkled with villages that they
are seldom far apart.   For another, the scenery is
purely English, with its green undulating landscape of arable, meadow and woodland, its cluster-
ing, red-roofed, spire-crowned villages ;   and to us
who have the blood of many English generations
in our veins, it must needs be satisfying, whether
we are conscious of it or not, to look upon scenes
such as those amid which our fathers' lives were
passed. I have felt this strongly in Essex, though

having no ties of kindred or early association with
it. Some have found the Essex country folk un-
sympathetic. This has not been my lot. Sometimes, looking back upon a holiday in their midst,
it has struck me that I had not met a single person
whom it was not a pleasure to know. The traveller
here, though he may be a perfect stranger, is
welcomed as an honoured guest. If one meets the
people frankly, likes their country, and enters into
their mode of life, they invariably respond. And
after all, as scenery, architecture, and the like are
mainly interesting for their bearing on human life,
so unless all human life has a charm for us its outward surroundings and manifestations can yield us
no true satisfaction.

I do not pretend to be the original discoverer of
Essex. I gratefully acknowledge that my interest
in it was first aroused by Mr Percy Lindley's little
handbook of " New Holidays. " Its local anti-
quaries have both knowledge and enthusiasm, but
the results of their labours are little known outside
the limits of the county. Most other writers who
mention Essex at all, either echo the public prejudice against it or damn it with faint praise.
That this was not always so, we learn from the
eulogium of John Norden in 1594 : " This shire,
is most fatt, frutefull, and full of profitable thinges,
exceeding (as far as I can finde) anie other shire,
for the generall comodeties, and the plentie.
Though Suffolke be more highlie comended of

8   An Undiscovered Country

some, wherwith I am not yet aquaynted : But
this shire seemeth to me to deserve the title of
the englishe Goshen, the fattest of the Lande :
comparable to Palestina, that flowed with milke
and hunnye. " Perhaps it will be urged that
old Norden's view is too gross and prosaic for
modern ideas, and that historic and legendary
interest is what we now look for. Well, I turn
to Timbs' " Abbeys and Castles of England and
Wales. " In this voluminous, I had almost said
exhaustive work, Essex is not even included.
In this thick darkness the rising generation also
is allowed to grope ; since " The Forty Shires, "
a work intended for the young, consisting of
several hundred pages, devotes less than one to
Essex. That it is a " much maligned county, "
as Walter White declared, is a reproach applicable to some who might have known better.
" As Butler says of Holland, it may be said of
Essex, " wrote the late Mackenzie Walcott, " that
it is like a large ship at anchor : there is a wild,
misty light, a neutral-tinted landscape, a silent
repose in those wide monotonous plains, dreary
and spacious, ever struggling with the ocean for
existence, land and sea of one colour, " etc., etc.
even Mr C. R. B. Barrett, who has produced two
charming volumes under the title of " Essex :
Highways, Byways, and Waterways, " ventures no
further at the outset than to recommend the
county as " rich in antiquarian interest, and not

deficient in natural beauty. " The press of this country, it is a truism to say, both guides and reflects public opinion : what is its verdict on Essex? The representative of a great daily newspaper, even when invited to Dunmow by that fairy genius of Essex, the Countess of Warwick, to report upon a technical school maintained by her, begins his article with unshaken fidelity to prejudice, by referring to Essex as " a county not too highly favoured either in the matter of natural beauty or fertility of soil. " Then the newer journalism takes its turn, and a writer of the dispirited realist type shows a ludicrous want of acquaintance with the sylvan recesses of the county, when, wandering about the marshes, he observes, " It is a pleasant lane *for Essex.* " Yet even he is forced to conclude : " Much as it has been abused, there is a romance and beauty still left in the Essex coast. " This confession is emphasised by the author of Cowper's " Sailing Tours, " who while chiefly interested in threading the maze of tidal rivers and navigable creeks, has an eye to what is to be found ashore, and exclaims : " This county is full of romance, it seems. " Mr Miller Christy's " Handbook for Essex " is, of course, by an Essex man, and in its way a classic. But from no source, perhaps, have I derived more enjoyment than from the Post Office Directory, a work hardly appreciated as it deserves. Sympathetically looked at, the seemingly dry facts it catalogues are full of life. Occasionally the prose rises into poetry, and the sober chronicler testifies that some village is " ancient and picturesque, " " beautifully situated. " or " surrounded by bold and romantic scenery. " But of course there are many books that help one to understand Essex which were written with no such intention. The best interpreter I know of the sentiment of English roads and wayfaring life is George Borrow, an ardent East Anglian ; and of mediæval England, William Morris, who was born at Walthamstow, and in his romance of the fourteenth century significantly styles himself " The Man from Essex."

Put together in odd intervals of leisure, this book cannot pretend to be a complete survey of the county. It is merely a frank record of personal impressions, intended for those who desire, without affection or merely conventional preference, to recognise natural beauty wherever it may be found, and are willing to take some little trouble in the search. I emulate neither the omniscience of the pocket cicerone, nor his infallibility of judgment as to what must or must not be admired. Nor shall I follow the literary fashions of writers whose imagination carries them further than mine. If I refrain from saying " I expected to see a mail-clad knight " or " to hear the solemn chant of the monks in the cloister, " it is because I never expect to see or hear these things. Topography is for me, as criticism for a recent writer, a branch of autobiography. " As I have felt, so I have written, " said the illustrious author of " Eothen. " " My narrative conveys — not those impressions which ought to have been produced upon any well-constituted mind, but those which were really and truly received at the time of my rambles. My notion is to dwell precisely upon those matters which happened to interest me, and upon none other. " Further, I must fortify myself with the authority of Hawthorne, who says that a truer impression of a scene or event may often be conveyed by an account of the feelings and ideas it evoked in the spectator than by pages of exact description. Finally, it is neither possible nor desirable for all of us to admire the same things. I want my readers to go and find fresh beauties in Essex for themselves. Hence I had great joy when an artist friend wrote to tell me that he had discovered a village which I had overlooked, and which appeared to him the most enrapturing he had ever seen.

II

The Art of Walking

" Happier life I cannot imagine than this vagrancy. " – *DeQuincey.*

" SOMEONE must be conservative enough, " says a recent writer, " to champion the disappearing art of walking. " I wish in this chapter to do battle in its behalf, especially as Essex can only be fully appreciated on foot. Indeed, in these days the pedestrian is in a hopeless minority. Cycling has no doubt its advantages : it is an exhilarating pastime ; it takes its votaries rapidly away from bricks and mortar, and enables them to go far in a day. But on the principle laid down by the Scotch professor that every advantage involves a corresponding disadvantage, the following draw-backs have to be reckoned. Cycling tempts the rider, for the sake of an even surface, to keep almost wholly to the high roads ; which is a dull proceeding, for it is only in the by-ways and out-of-the-way corners that what is really characteristic is to be found. A constant stream of traffic wears down the natural and the social features of a district ; and hence all high roads are more or less alike. That every hill shall be made low and every valley exalted, as the ancient prophecy declares, is undoubtedly the goal of engineering ; but it is surely more as a cyclist than as an artist that Mr Joseph Pennell commends the road-makers of the continent for cutting off the tops of the hills and filling up the valleys with the material so obtained. A pedestrian is free to take in everything around him, when his fellow on wheels is intent upon the surface of the road or on the speed at which he can traverse it. In a sedentary age, the danger of breaking one's neck, either by the recklessness of one's self or of others should perhaps be counted for righteousness ; but where is the virtue in punctures and such minor mishaps ? In mounting hills, just when additional weight is least wanted, a machine is simply an incumbrance. No ; though conscious of being but a voice crying in the wilderness, I must repeat the self-evident truth that walking is the normal means of progression. Nature has given it her blessing. Demanding an upright carriage, filling the lungs with pure air, and bringing all the muscles of the body into play, it is the ideal exercise, and the best physic I know. For the cure of any of the nervous ills of modern life, give me twenty-four hours with my feet on the gravel or the grass. Essex is a pedestrian's paradise. The vistas of its winding and gently undulating roads are an unflagging stimulus to exertion, its wayside trees and hedgerows give plenty of shade and shelter, and its hostelries afford good entertainment.

Walking is the best way of seeing the country. " Whether we like it or not, " says the writer with whose words I began this chapter, " Nature has decreed that we must approach her shrine on foot, at a pace of not more than two-and-a-half or three miles an hour. " But walking is an art ; and like every other art, it must be learned. Not everyone is equal to it. Many young and vigorous people, accustomed to athletic exercise, find themselves hard put to it when called upon to accomplish a steady twenty miles a day. The knack of endurance must be acquired. The primary requisite is, of course, a pair of stout, yet easy, shoes. In the matter of *impedimenta*, one must steer between the Scylla of overburdening one's back and the Charybdis of sacrificing reasonable personal comfort. As a precaution against rain, an ample cape of light, yet closely-woven cloth is better than a mackintosh, as it gives equal protection with far greater ease. It is well, before starting, to form some idea of the route to be taken, and the points of interest to be looked for ; and every evening in the course of a journey it will be found useful as well as amusing to work out in detail, with the aid of a map, the itinerary for the morrow. " The little black dots and lines become wonderfully interesting when you mean to go and see what those symbols represent, "

says an Essex explorer ; and reading the meaning
of maps is an art in itself. Having settled on
the district to be studied, supposing it to lie near
London, do not make the mistake of walking
through uninteresting suburbs, but take the train
to some convenient point, so that your ramble
may begin in pure air and amid fresh surroundings. Have in your mind some town or large
village (preferably one that has seen better days)
where you think it would be pleasant to pass the night,
and aim to reach it about sunset. As a
rule, throughout Essex, good " commercial " inns
are the best to choose. In such houses there are
traditions, so to speak, of goodwill towards the
traveller, which must be felt to be appreciated. I
have often become so attached to an inn and its
people as to feel positive sorrow at leaving them —
in which travel is an allegory of life. Entering the
cosy kitchen or parlour, you are received with
the utmost friendliness by its convivial circle of
frequenters. Often noisy and sometimes unintelligible, to the sympathetic observer the talk of the
local people is racy and interesting to a degree.
In the matter of meals the novice has much to
learn. If the business of walking be seriously
undertaken, the whole day must be given to it,
and the midday repast must be a modest one.
Bread and cheese and ale make a good substitute,
and can be had anywhere at a moment's notice.
On arriving in the evening at a satisfactory inn, a

meal may be ordered which shall be as substantial as the resources of the establishment will permit. Breakfast, to which full justice should be done, follows in due course ; and thus the traveller is spared the time and trouble which would otherwise be wasted in hunting for food during the day. Meat or eggs, bread and tea, may not seem a very liberal diet, but it is the most sustaining of all in the end. Following this system, the walker is really undergoing a process of training, and soon becomes fit for any exertion. To me, this manner of living is an ideal one ; and the cost of it but a few shillings a day.

A word now as to the best time of year for a walking tour. Easter is a favourite season with me : the weather is then usually clear and cold, so that exercise is a pleasure ; the sense of spring is exhilarating, and, in the evening, one is sure of finding a fire at the inn, which is a great charm. In early and mid-summer there are flowers, the wild roses and honeysuckle, and the hayfields : at harvest-time, the opulent acres of golden-brown corn and the incessant whirr of the reaper in the quivering heat. Then there are the still days of early autumn, with the blue morning haze over the woodlands, the clusters of ripened fruit in garden and orchard, the feast of blackberries everywhere. In finding one's way across the country, the sun and the time of the day together make a rough but trustworthy guide to the points of the compass.

Henham-on-the-Hill — The Cock Inn.

Mountnessing — Windmill.

The ideal day for walking is perhaps one of those which are so welcome after rain : the air is fresh and cool, and the wind makes a pleasant music in the trees that border the way ;   large white clouds slowly travel over the sky, and cast their moving shadows across the landscape :   on such days the shifting sunlight picks out distant objects with surprising clearness.

The great charm of a pedestrian holiday is its freedom. You throw aside time-tables and all forms of constraint. You enter into the spirit of Whitman's joyous burst of song:—

" Afoot and light-hearted I take to the open road,
   Healthy, free, the world before me,
   The long brown path before me leading wherever I choose. "

This sense of freedom is essential to true ped-estrianism. Hence it is usually a mistake to fix upon any one place, even for two or three days, as a sort of headquarters or centre ;   for although by such means one is relieved from the trouble of carrying one's belongings about, yet the feeling that one must return each day to a given spot becomes irksome. So also as to travelling com-panions. To accompany a friend upon a walking journey is to put your friendship to the severest test. " Can two walk together, except they be agreed ? "   I would a hundred times rather have no companion than an uncongenial one. Nature should be society enough, if need be, for any man. Not that we can always, when in her presence, be in that exalted mood of which Emerson speaks, when he says :— " Crossing a bare common, in snow puddles, at twilight, under a clouded sky, without having in my thoughts any occurrence of special good fortune, I have enjoyed a perfect exhilaration. Almost I fear to think how glad I am. " yet at all times " the air is a cordial of incredible virtue. " " The trick is, I find, " says Whitman, one of the subtlest of observers, " to tone your wants and tastes low down enough, and to make much of negatives, and of mere daylight and the skies. " Why should we always expect Nature to be melodramatic ? It is the brand of artificiality. Our children are wiser. Once in the first days of March, I promised my boy a country ramble, but warned him that it was too early in the year to look for flowers. " Never mind, " he said, " there will be grass and paths. " Yet as even a pedestrian may feel dull sometimes, it is well that he should have an object in view. what can be better than an interest in architecture ? Rich in that, he will cheerfully traverse miles of stony road to feast his eyes upon some artistic bit of ancient building ; while, should the landscape smile sweetly upon him, as it almost surely will, its beauty is a free and unasked-for gift. With what joy he sees, at a turn of the road, some massive grey church tower, surrounded by a cluster of red roofs, crowning the distant hill, or the silvery gleam of some slender spire among the trees in the valley ! Then at the end of the day he may feel, as Pater felt, " that indescribable sense of welcoming in the mere outward appearance of things, which seems to mark out certain places for the special purpose of evening rest, and gives them always a peculiar amiability in retrospect. Under the deepening twilight, the rough-tiled roofs seem to huddle together side by side, like one continuous shelter over the whole township, spread low and broad above the snug sleeping-rooms within ; and the place one sees for the first time, and must tarry in but for a night, breathes the very spirit of home."

III

Footpaths and Green Lanes

" Never was there a footpath yet which did not pass something of interest. "– *Jefferies.*

" To see England, to know in the least the heart of the country we are so proud to call our own, it is necessary to leave the beaten track entirely, and plunge into any by-path that may look appealingly at us, and make our way into that dim mysterious land that that is so near us, and yet might be non-existent for all that the generality of folks know of its existence. " Perhaps the want of appreciation to which the writer refers may be due to the fact that to us in England footpaths are so much in the natural order of things that we simply take them for granted. Yet they are undoubtedly among our most precious possessions ; not only for their own sake, but for their significance, as a mark of the mellowness of our civilisation and of the practical give-and-take of our national spirit. There is no other country in the world in which footpaths, as we understand them, are to be found. Foreign visitors express their astonishment when they see them. Our American cousins left them behind when the *Mayflower* sailed, and express unbounded surprise and delight at finding them here again. As a well-known writer from the States put it, they make the old country look like one large garden.

The antiquity of footpaths is undoubted. It is quite certain that the famous path from Stratford-on-Avon to Shottery existed in the time of Shakespeare, and he probably followed it hundreds of times in the days when he wooed Anne Hathaway. This gives for us an added charm to the lilt which he puts into the mouth of Autolycus:

" Jog on, jog on the footpath way,
    And merrily hent the stile-a;
A merry heart goes all the day,
    Your sad tires in a mile-a. "

But innumerable paths must have existed much longer than the three centuries which have elapsed since Shakespeare wrote. Some of them are probably as old as anything in these islands. The rights of way which still exist across private parks suggest that in most cases the paths themselves were in common use long before the parks were enclosed.

Footpaths give an opportunity, such as nothing else affords, for intimate acquaintance with the country. Shy wild creatures that shun the roads may often be startled from their hiding-places ; and blossoms and berries which merely struggle for existence elsewhere grow here in profusion.

Not only so ;   the husbandman takes you into his confidence.   You may open his heavy gate and go through his rick-yard.   A narrow passage is left for you across his carefully-ploughed acres.   You skirt a field of sweet-scented pea-blossom of all colours, or admire his growing corn as you pass through the midst of it waist or shoulder high and let the ears slip through your hand as you go.   If your way lies along the meadows of some river valley you encounter the herdsman's cattle ;   or climbing some stony upland, the nibbling sheep scatter at your approach.   The path descends as it nears a brook ; you cross the brook by a narrow bridge — perhaps merely a split tree trunk, with the rounded side undermost — laid there you know not by whom. The running water has worn for itself a deep channel through the soft loam till it reaches the gravel over which it runs.   The path follows the stream ;   but its banks are overgrown with luxuriant bushes so that you cannot see the stream although you hear its music.   The bushes spread into a wood of trees ;   through this the path unerringly runs, until, emerging from the cool shade of the boughs, you see the track continued across the fields again.   Sometimes the track is difficult to follow, or splits up into several ways ;   but with practice you acquire a sort of instinct which points out the right one, and which may be called " the footpath sense. "   Paths are of all kinds.   Sometimes they are broad and unmistakable — therefore less interesting. At other times the narrow brown streak grows fainter, until the only sign of a path is a slight discolouration of the grass. What impresses me most about them is the kindly feeling they convey. You may be traversing a lonely district, and meet never a soul, but on the footpath you are expected and your coming is prepared for. Sometimes, in crossing a field, no gap is visible opposite in the overgrown hedge ; but just as you reach it you find the hidden stile, and a wooden step stands ready to your foot. Occasionally you may be reminded of Fuller's commemoration of " the height of Essex stiles " as you encounter one that calls for climbing ; and you will note that the lowest bar is always the thinnest because it is the hardest used. A stile is always an encouragement and a sign that you are at least on a recognised path, which is sure to lead you somewhere. Indeed, as a rule, the footpath is not only the pleasantest but the shortest way between two points of human habitation. Two villages with a footpath between them—that for me, is England.

" Always get over a stile, " said Jefferies. But while stiles are an incident of footpaths, there are footpaths without stiles, namely, green lanes. I do not mean the green " rides " of Epping Forest, where a broad turfy road leads through the woodlands, into which at any point you may wander if you will ; but the grassy thoroughfares that are still to be traced about the country, often in the near neighbourhood of towns. Frequently it will be found that they offer a directer route than the modern roads between place and place. For many of these old grassy thoroughfares, full of ruts and holes, are really old mediæval roads fallen into desuetude and consequently not improved. They therefore give one a very fair impression of what such roads were really like — road-making being one of the few practical arts in which we have done better than the middle ages. Some towns and villages having risen in prosperity, while others have fallen, the course of the main thoroughfares has been changed ; so that it is no uncommon thing nowadays to find little lonely hamlets, consisting of a dozen houses and a church, connected by old roads whose width alone is a sign of their former volume of traffic. In some instances they are still pleasantly bordered by ancient trees on either hand. Here and there you may even see a green lane in process of making. A road, once of some importance, now leads perhaps only to a secluded farm. The substance of the road is visible only in three long white strips — a broad one down the middle, worn by the feet of the farmer's horses, and two narrower ones at the side where the wheels of his light trap or heavy waggon run without meeting anything to cause them to turn aside. The rest of the road is overgrown with grass.

The special charm of green lanes is this. You

enter and leave them without hindrance. They are are as free to you as the public roads, being themselves roads to such as care to use them. The broad strip of greensward stretches before you, a field among the fields, where you find quiet without trespass. They are beloved of gipsies, or of such of this strange tribe remain. was it not in a green lane near Norman Cross that George Borrow as a boy had his first encounter with the Egyptians ? Here " he fell in with a low tent from which smoke was issuing, and in front of which a man was plaiting carded straw, while a woman was engaged in the manufacture of spurious coin. Their queer appearance, so unlike that of any men or women he had hitherto encountered, excited his lively curiosity ; but, ere he had time to examine them closely, they were down upon him with threats and curses. Violence was about to be done to him when a viper, which he had concealed in his jacket, lifted its head from his bosom, and the gipsies' wrath at being discovered changed to awe of one who fearlessly handled such a deadly creature. " An adventure of this kind is little likely to befall anyone to-day ; but itinerants of various types may often be met with, their cooking-pot on the fire, garments drying on the hedge, and generally some half-dozen lean horses wandering in search of pasture. Once in a green lane I dined, in company with a travelling tinker and his wife, upon a sheep's head, a dainty which I have never tasted since except at a club in Edinburgh. But far oftener than you come across these homeless wanderers you will find traces of their fires. An old fire is known by a black circle on the grass. If the fire be recent the circle will be white. Lay your hands upon the ashes. Perhaps an unexpected heat in the seemingly dead embers will apprise you that the encampment has been but a few hours broken up. Sometimes a sharp stick will be found with one end thrust obliquely in the earth, the other inclined over the fire, and the middle supported by a large stone or a forked branch. This is the primitive roasting-jack. Most of these camping-spots are admirably chosen ; screened from the wind by the bushes, which grow unchecked in green lanes, and near little streams of running water. It is strange to note, after centuries of life in cities and settled communities, what small things may serve to remind us that the old nomadic instincts in our blood are not dead, but sleeping.

IV

Among the Chalk Hills

" Familiar remoteness. "

The little cluster of hills shown by lines of vigorous black shading in the north-west corner of the map of Essex had long fascinated my imagination. So, at the end of a brief but delightful visit to a friend at Ashwell in Hertfordshire, I shook him by the hand, and turned my face, like the pilgrims of old, towards the east. Reaching Royston about noon, I pressed forward until I struck the ancient British road known as the Icknield Way — a name which recalls the tribe of Iceni, of whom Boadicea was queen. As everyone knows, the ancient British roads differ entirely from those bequeathed to us by the Romans. These invaders, true to their habitual thoroughness and military precision, and heedless whether their stay in our island were to be long or short, constructed magnificent roads to render communication and transport easy between their fortified posts ; and in constructing them, whatever natural obstacles they might encounter, they

27

adhered as nearly as possible to a straight line. The early Celtic inhabitants, on the contrary, seem to have carried their principal paths or " ridge-ways " along the tops of the highest hills, partly for the sake of dryness, but chiefly, no doubt, to protect them against the sudden approach of an enemy by affording a wide view of the surrounding country. To avoid observation in moving from place to place, the roads were sometimes sunk some feet below the natural level of the ground in the form of a ditch or dyke. It was, then, with great delight that I found myself following this prehistoric thoroughfare, which leads now to no place of any importance, and saw it winding and stretching away into the distance over the hills. For several hours I followed it, hardly meeting a human being or seeing any sign of human habitation, until I could almost fancy that the road led only into the regions of the past. On and on I went, until day drew towards evening, and I began to think I should be benighted upon this wild deserted way. At length there appeared far away upon the right a line of dark woods that looked as though some village lay sheltered be-hind them ; and on the left, but much nearer, the roofs and smoking chimneys of what I took to be a little village or hamlet. Choosing the latter direction, being tired and hungry, my surprise was great when my fancied village proved to be nothing more than the straggling buildings of a great solitary farm or grange. Near the farm was a cottage, the door of which stood open ; and in answer to my question, the housewife said that the nearest village was three miles away. However, seeing my plight, she herself prepared tea for me ; but when I rose to go, she would accept no payment for her hospitality, and was with difficulty induced to take it as gift for her child. Had I not really wandered out of the world?

Now up the opposite hill I climbed, to find the village hidden behind the trees. Arriving presently at a sign-post pointing one way to Elmdon, and the other to Heydon, I consulted the map and chose the latter road ; yet when, just after dusk, I reached a pretty village on the slope of a hill, I found that it was Elmdon after all. How it happened I never could guess; nor did I greatly care when ensconced in the long low room of a comfortable inn, the lights in the antique silver candlesticks gleaming on a snowy cloth spread with dainty and substantial fare.

All the next day I wandered by lanes and grassy paths up and down a hilly, well-wooded country, passing here and there some stately house standing solitary upon a height surrounded by its trees and moat. In one place there were two moats in the midst of a wood, from which the wild-fowl rose startled at my approach. At sunset I reached

Henham-on-the Hill, a village whose name sounded
interesting, and one which I had often tried to
realise in imagination ; though, as usually happens,
the imaginary picture proved to be very little like
the reality.   Can the reader see with his mind's
eye a broad plateau traversed by broad shady
roads which divide green expanses of common
around which are scattered a number of idyllic
cottages mostly roofed with thatch ?   There are
plenty of thatched houses, of course, in Essex;
but as a rule there is not a large proportion of
them in any one village.   This is one peculiarity of
Henham.   It is very nearly, if not quite unspoilt.   The church stands boldly at the end of
the village where the road branches off, and opposite
swings the sign of the principal inn.

One day that I spent in this lonely region among
the chalk hills I shall never forget.   It was Sunday,
I remember, as I approached a little upland village.
As is often seen in chalky district, the land was
in some parts perfectly bare of timber, its bold
curving lines showing naked against the sky, while
now and then the road skirted a wood of such
thickness that it seemed impossible to penetrate it,
even with the eye.   The white roads glistened in
the strong sunlight.   It was past noon when the
first houses were reached.   I was weary, hungry and
thirsty; but the village could boast no house
of entertainment.   Another and more hospitable
hamlet was pointed out to me upon the opposite

hill, and I soon made my way to it, following a footpath down the slope and then up through several fields. Entering the kitchen of the little ale-house, which was roughly furnished with wooden tables and benches, and expecting only the coarsest of fare, to my great surprise I was served in a short time with a chop, perfectly cooked, accompanied by fresh vegetables from the garden. More than this, I was the witness of a very amusing little comedy. Several young fellows, apparently of the farming class, were drinking copious draughts of what seemed to be weak whisky and water ready mixed in a jug, which the young landlord was kept constantly carrying backward and forward. It was harvest time, and one of the men went round with the jug, saying, " Drink up, " and persistently pressing the liquor upon the others, who rather shame-facedly accepted it. The conversation turned upon " closing time, " and the police, one youth boasting how he had once out-brazened the officer of the law, or as he expressed it in choice vernacular, " He didn't take no notice of me, and I didn't take no notice of he." The land-lord grew uneasy and glanced more than once at the clock; his face expressed the conflict going on within him between respect for the law and the desire to conciliate good customers. However, the drinking party soon slouched off, and the little comedy ended.

Returning by the fields, I reached the church in time for afternoon service. A visit there from a stranger must be a rare occurrence, for my entrance aroused the curiosity of the whole congregation; while several of them eyed me furtively all the time, as though speculating on the reason for my coming. The church consisted only of chancel and nave ; indeed, it was so small that it was nearly full, although hardly more than twenty people were present. The arch dividing nave from chancel was semi-circular in form, of Norman design, bold and impressive. Beneath it, the clergyman, a man advanced in years, delivered a discourse which, whatever its merits, had certainly not the simplicity of his audience and surroundings. On my right sat a man with his children, evidently a labourer, yet whose face bore such traces of thought and refinement, that I could hardly take my eyes from him. In that remote spot, amid the stillness of that hour, the house of God built by the fervour of a bygone age, framing the restless rustic congregation, the droning cleric, and the face of this simple yet noble man, formed a picture which will be forever stamped upon my memory.

Strethall — The Church of St Mary the Virgin.

Saffron Walden — The Sun Inn.

V

The Watershed of Essex

" The past is the heirloom of the world." – *Leigh Hunt*

THAT summer Sabbath day was drawing to its close, and the westering sky shone warmly upon the trees and the tall spire above them as I crossed the bridge into the quiet streets of Saffron Walden. Yet here I was destined to be inhospitably entertained. At house after house I received the tidings that it was impossible to accommodate me for the night. This happened so often that I almost determined to shake off the dust of Saffron Walden. from my feet, and push on through the dusk of the evening to Radwinter ; but I thought better of it. I reflected that I had been tramping all day in the hot sun, and that my appearance must leave something to be desired. It was near the hour of evening service, and my arrival at that time was perhaps inconsiderate. Inhabitants of country towns have their prejudices, which are entitled to respect ; at least I have learned to respect them. These good people had taught me a lesson in manners. I hasten to add that this untoward

C

experience, as it was my first of the kind, has also been the last.   But I have felt ever since that Saffron Walden is rather in Essex than of it.

Like many another homeless wanderer, I stole for the second time that day into that refuge of the homeless, the church.   Resting in a quiet corner, I watched the last rays of sunlight travel round the lofty piers, and listened to the music and the soothing cadences of the liturgy, until things began to resume their right proportions, and it seemed to matter very little whether I secured a night's lodging or not.

Later in the evening I obtained, without trouble, comfortable quarters in the town, and in the morning was ready to explore the place in a Christian spirit.   Notwithstanding the somewhat cold and formal air of some of its streets, I found its general aspect interesting and pleasing, with many old houses of timber and plaster, and several ancient inns, one of which, the *Sun*, was Cromwell's headquarters here.   First I climbed to the top of Windmill Hill to take in the town as a whole. Next, I made my way to the earthworks locally known as the Battle Ditches.   It was pleasant to find in this flourishing commercial centre the rectangular plan of the Roman fortification still plainly to be traced.   It enclosed, I found, a considerable part of the present town.   A path ran along the top of the rampart for some distance, overlooking the deep ditch below.   Many relics of the Roman occupation have been recovered, and are preserved in the museum, with iron and bronze implements, and skeletons from a neighbouring spot which has been identified as a Saxon burial-ground.

At Bury Hill, the highest point of the town, a castle existed in Saxon times, founded by Anscar, master of the horse to King Edward the Confessor. When the Normans took possession of the country , this stronghold passed into the hands of the celebrated Geoffrey de Mandeville, who rebuilt the castle on the same plan as that of the more famous fortress at Hedingham, some miles to the east. Nothing now remains but the ivy-clad foundation walls, which once formed the donjon, standing to a height of about twenty-five feet.

The church of Saffron Walden is imposing without and within. Like many of the churches of the Late Perpendicular epoch, it compels admiration by its spaciousness, lofty design, and general prevalence of light and air. and yet, like all buildings of the same age, it seems to me to lack something. It has admirable qualities, yet it leaves you cold. Its absolute mastery of material conveys a hint of materialism. In the development from the simpler and ruder forms of architecture, it has lost much of the old mystery and romance. Carved in the spandrels of the aisle arch opposite the south door are saffron flowers. This reminds us that the saffron crocus was once largely grown around the town, from which fact its present prefix is derived. Few names of places tell their own story so plainly. " Walden " — the town among woods — was the graphic term applied by the Saxons, who prefixed the word " Chipping " to indicate the existence of a market. The substitution of " Saffron " corresponds with later events. Saffron being no longer grown here now, the town is again spoken of simply as Walden, which root name has probably always sufficed for its inhabitants.

Close to the borders of the town stretches the park of Audley End. The house of this name is looked upon as the most magnificent residence in Essex. Yet the history of Audley End — like that of many of the great houses in Essex — is rather saddening, if instructive, to those who take an intelligent interest in their country's past. The builder of the castle at Walden, Geoffrey de Mandeville, only followed the usual custom of Norman lords when he founded and endowed a religious house hard by. A mile to the west of the town, in a sheltered valley of the river Cam, arose in 1146 the walls of the Benedictine priory. Here for centuries went on that quiet routine of service so indispensable in the economy of the Middle Ages — the offices of learning and religion, relief of the sick and needy, entertainment of travellers — until the time came when the sloth and avarice that were eating away the heart of monastic institutions from within were to be swept away by a greater violence and greed from without. The abbey perished in the Dissolution, and its lands and buildings passed into the hands of the Lord Chancellor, Sir Thomas Audley. Crafty and sycophantic with the strong, relentless and cruel to the weak, at all times intent on his own aggrandisements, this man was one of the typical courtiers of the age. " Cormorants, " they were called by Henry, who was nothing if not plain spoken, and who, while he used them to serve his purposes, felt for them a hearty contempt, which we cannot but share. The sacred buildings were pulled down by Audley to make room for a private mansion befitting the new scheme of things ; but it was his grandson, the first Earl of Suffolk, who erected, at fabulous cost, the enormous buildings of which the present lordly house is but a renovated fragment. Surrounded by the river, with beautiful trees and acres of faultless lawn, the house to-day with its wealth of pictures, carvings and artistic treasures of all kinds, is of course closed to the public. Curiously enough, the stables of the modern establishment are a sole remaining portion of the original priory, that portion which was once the hostel, whose doors stood open to all comers. Even the admirable personal qualities of the present owners of the estate do not quite enable us to contemplate its history without regret.

The park at Audley End is divided from north to south by a great high road from Cambridge to London. A few miles to the south lies Newport, which should certainly be visited for the sake of the wonderful old houses that stand in its single street. One of them, called Monk Barns, believed to have belonged to some religious fraternity, has upon its front a carved wooden group of figures which seem to represent the coronation of the Virgin. Not far off stands the Crown House (so called from a crown over the door), said to have been formerly occupied by Nell Gwynne ; while the *Coach and Horses* Inn also has associations with the reign in which she flourished.

Northward, the road passes through Great Chesterford, now nothing but a large village, dominated by a church chiefly of Perpendicular date, and encircled by the windings of the Cam. This place is the ancient Camboritum, one of a chain of Roman forts stretching from Newmarket to the Forest of Essex. The Saxon name of the place describes the ford over the river by the Roman fortress. Traces of entrenchments still remain, and numberless Roman relics have been brought to light.

Turning eastward we reach the scattered village of Ashdon, which has many thatched cottages, and, in the churchyard, an old house inhabited in pre-Reformation days by the priest. But the chief claim of this place to renown is an imaginary one. although its name appears in a legal document of the reign of Edward III. in the guise of " Ascendune, " the site of the famous battle fought in

1016 it certainly is not. Its title to this honour rested largely on the belief that the barrows of Bartlow, two miles away, were the graves of Danish chiefs ; but the barrows were opened and their contents proved to be much older than the date of the battle. Nor does the lie of the ground here suggest a battlefield; while the hill at Ashingdon in the east seems made by nature for that purpose.

The terror which we know the Danes inspired by their fierce and sudden incursions, carrying sword and fire through the land, may throw some light on the persistent tendency of later generations to attribute to this race the barrows, mounds, and any prominent objects the meaning of which was doubtful. They appear to have become a sort of national bogey, as Bonaparte was within the present century. An instance of this occurs at Hadstock, distant from Ashdon but a few miles. Here, the north door of the church was until lately covered with human skin, doubtless that of some one who had robbed the sanctuary, a crime which in early times entailed a fearful punishment of flaying alive ; but, beyond the mythical tendency of which we are speaking, there seems no ground for the tradition that the offender was a Dane. The stout old oaken door has still innumerable holes from the nails by which the skin was stretched over it. Entering the church through the Norman doorway, one cannot fail to be struck

by a certain largeness and boldness in the piers
and round arches at the centre of the cruciform
plan in contrast with the modest size of the building as a whole.   Perhaps it was meant to be
something more than a simple village church.   It
was probably finished on a smaller scale than was
at first intended ;   at all events, the central tower,
which would have been its crowning glory, was
never built.   As we pass through the churchyard,
which contains a stone well, dedicated, like the
church, to Saint Botolph, the primitive village
rises before us, with its inns at the diverging
roads, its thatched cottages piled in picturesque
confusion, and an old gabled house at the summit.
Entering one of the inns to taste the ale of the
district and get speech with the hostess, the
rafters of the kitchen are barely above my head,
and upon them may easily be deciphered the
Roman numerals rudely cut there by the chisel
of some bygone craftsman, who doubtless framed
the whole dwelling before he set a single beam of
it in position.

A neighbouring hamlet of rather similar type
is Bartlow.   Here we encounter the railway, but
somehow it blends with its surroundings, and is
hardly felt as an intrusion.   a bridge carries the
line across the road ;   just beyond it the road dips,
and one of those little clear streams it is always
delightful to meet goes merrily over the stones,
winding out of one field through a gap in the

hedge, and into the opposite field in like manner, spanned by a bridge of planks for the convenience of foot passengers. The church here is an interesting one, with a round tower, and a faded fresco of Saint Christopher over the south door. But the chief charm of the place is found in the barrows or Bartlow Hills as they are called, which stand on the boundary line that separates Essex from Cambridgeshire. At their foot are traces of a Roman camp ; where, when I visited the place, agricultural digging was going on, and fragments of Samian and other pottery were being thrown up by the spade. The aspect of these mounds is like that of nothing else in Essex. There are four of them, ranged close together in a row, not all of the same size, but each in form an almost perfect dome.

" In 1835, " says Mr A R Goddard, " the largest and highest of the group was tunnelled, and traces of a small cell of timber were found with important contents. These made it clear that the grave belonged to a personage of note, and were as follows : glass vessels and long phials containing, probably, unguents, of which the larger portion remained, although somewhat metamorphosed ; two fine bronze strigils (used in the Roman bath) ; a folding-stool with bronze frame, and remnants of a former seat and back of leather ; a fine bronze patera, and a graceful pitcher with ornament in silver inlay ; a bronze lamp with richly-wrought acanthus leaf for handle ; a unique little incense-pot of bronze, with design in overlay of red, blue, and green enamel ; and last, the cremated bone deposit in a green glass bottle of similar shape to the one already described, but larger ”   in another of the barrows was found “ a walled tomb, built and covered in with Roman brick.   When the top was removed, the deposits were found intact, as laid more than seventeen centuries before.   Among the objects in this tomb were a brass coin of Hadrian, and a gold ring with an intaglio of two bearded ears of wheat, a symbol often found on the coins of Cunobelin, and his father, Tasciovanus. ”   It is considered probable “ that these barrows were the memorials of notables of British birth, reared by friends and associates who followed the custom of their forefathers as to the form of their monuments, whilst adopting the prevailing fashion of deposits from their rulers and conquerors.   Does some cherished descent from the famous line of Cunobelin lie implied in the deposit of the intaglio with the royal symbol?”

Climb the steep side of one of these hills — the highest is seventy feet — and stand among the wind-swept trees at the top.   From hence you may survey, as men of one race after another have for centuries surveyed, the landscape that spreads around, traversed in all directions by the roads of the Roman generals.   This cluster of chalk hills may be called the water-shed of Essex ; for within them nearly all the streams that find their way through the county take their rise. To the north-west can be seen the bluff Gog-Magog hills, where a high modern authority is inclined to place the site of ancient Camalodunum. But the balance of evidence seems to be with the learned majority who tell us that for that intensely interesting spot we must look elsewhere : eastward from where we stand, down the valley of the Colne, to COL-CHESTER, whither our steps must now be directed.

VI

The Spell of Colchester

" Towns also and cities, especially the ancient, I failed not to look
upon with interest. " — *Carlyle*

As you approach Colchester over the breezy heaths
of Fordham and Bergholt that overlook the valley
of the Stour on the one hand and that of the Colne
on the other, your first distant view of the town
will very likely be a disappointment.   Its noble
situation is undeniable ;   the bold yet wide hill, on
which it stands, compelling the river to curve right
round it in its progress towards the further marshes
and the sea, and the railway to take an even wider
sweep.   But its ancient tiled roofs and church towers
are intermingled with the chimneys of factories and
the cold blue slate of the newer streets ;   and the
whole town is dominated from its most commanding
height not by the grey fretted spire of a stately
cathedral but by a brick structure of doubtful
architecture which you learn to be a water tower.
     This impression is not at once removed from the
mind of the visitor when he enters the town and
saunters through its principal streets.   Here and
there he will come across interesting old houses

44

and a well-preserved inn or two of the coaching age;   but signs will be abundant that the mere sentiment of antiquity has not been allowed to stand in the way of commercial progress.   Old houses are still being pulled down to make room for others more fitted to stand in the streets of a thriving provincial town, which is just what Colchester at first sight proclaims itself to be.   Yet one calls to mind that this place is one of the very earliest of which our annals make mention, and that its origin and early history are full of legendary interest.   That Constantine the Great was born in its precincts, and that to him and to his mother Helena it owed most of its greatness, was the firm belief of its inhabitants probably long before the Normans set foot amongst them — a belief which is perpetuated in the arms of the town to this day. The story went that Helena was the daughter of a certain British king named Coel (the " old king Cole " of our nursery recollections), who had his stronghold here, and successfully withstood the assaults of the Roman general Constantius ;   but that the king dying without a son to succeed him, his daughter Helena was wedded by Constantius, and that they reigned together at Colchester, where their son, the celebrated Constantine, was born.   Now it takes nothing from the interest of this tale to know from history that it cannot in fact be true.   The origin of the legend, as expounded by the ablest historian of Colchester, is an interesting example of the formation of myth. " It was natural enough that the Saxon burgesses should connect with the massive walls and ruined buildings of the ancient city amidst which they lived all their vague reminiscences of the races which had preceded them. They vaguely knew that it had been the royal town of British kings, and that it had been taken by a Roman emperor. They wanted a name for the British king, and they took it from the name of the place, Colchester, the castle of King Coel. Constantine the Great was the typical Roman emperor, and Constantine's mother was well known to have been Helena, the discoverer of the true cross. It needed but little of the spirit of historical romance to weave out of those materials a story which should shed lustre upon their town. "

Even without the aid of legend, the early history of this place, as we learn it from the pages of sober chroniclers like Seutonius and Tacitus, is full of romantic interest. It can be almost certainly identified as the *oppidum* or fortified enclosure of the Trinobantes described by Cæsar, as seen by him on his first landing in Britain. At the opening of the Christian era we get a glimpse of it as the royal town of Cunobelin (the Cymbeline of Shakespeare), many of whose coins have been recovered from the soil on which they were minted, and can be easily deciphered. After the subjugation of the southern tribes of Britain by Claudius in A.D. 44 he founded here a *Colonia* or colony of veterans. They cultivated the lands allotted to them, and a town arose, with theatres, temples, baths, and all the outward signs of Roman civilisation, under the name — a Latinised version of an early British one — Camulodunum. These men, Tacitus tells us, treated the Britons with cruelty and oppression, and thereby provoked them to a revolt, which was rendered easier by the false security in which the conquerors lived. " The Roman generals, " he says, " embellished the province with elegant improvements, but neglected to defend it. The colony had but a handful of soldiers. Unguarded and unprepared, they were taken by surprise. The colony was laid waste with fire and sword. " The avenging spirit of this rebellion was Boadicea, the widowed queen, her daughters ravished by the aliens, and herself disgraced with stripes — one of the most pathetic and heroic figures in all history. But the fierce spirit which her burning eloquence aroused in the hearts of the Britons was of no avail against the disciplined legion which hastened to meet them under the command of Suetonius. A single battle sufficed to crush the revolt for ever. Colonia Camulodunum rose again from its ashes. Effectual measures were taken to prevent a repetition of the disaster which had once overtaken it. It was perhaps at this time that the walls were raised. The historian, Freeman, is inclined to date them some two centuries later, from the time of Constantine.   But, he adds :   " The walls are there, whoever built them. . . . These walls are, as far as I have seen, unique among the inhabited towns of Britain. Neither York, nor Lincoln, nor Exeter, nor even Chester, can boast of being still girded by her Roman walls in anything like the same perfection in which Colchester is. . . .   While the circuit of the walls is much more perfect than at York and Lincoln, the fragments which still remain at York and Lincoln have kept much more of their ancient masonry than can be found at Colchester.   Still Colchester can show far more than can be seen at Chester, where, though the Roman lines are all but perfectly followed by the later defences, little is left of the actual Roman wall beyond its foundation.   As the abiding wall of a still in-habited town, the Roman wall of Colchester is, I repeat, unique in Britain."

We now begin to pierce the modern disguise which Colchester wears, and to see something of its hidden wonders.   Though High Street and Head Street, its principal thoroughfares, follow, north to south and east to west, the lines of the Roman thoroughfares, their aspect reveals to us nothing of their origin.   But as we pass outside the confines of the town at St Botolph's gate, or rather the site of it, and turn to the left along Priory Street, the ancient wall is to be seen;   and from this point it may be followed almost without

Colchester — The Water Tower.

Colchester — The Balkerne Gate.

a break round its whole circuit, an irregular parallelogram of about three thousand yards. In some places, as Freeman says, " the walls stand free ; everywhere they can be seen by going down courts and alleys. " In spite of the battering and patching of fifteen or eighteen centuries, even the original method of construction is clearly shown. Four courses of septaria — stone found in large quantities along the Essex coast — alternate with three layers of the thin Roman bricks. Thicker by several feet at the base than at the summit, the wall slopes up from the ground, the line of which it follows, the grey mass of its surface beautifully relieved by the warm red bands of brick, and by the ivy and moss that overrun it. In Priory Street, where our circuit begins, the houses, which are little more than cottages, are built just without and under the wall, which therefore appears plainly wherever there is a break in the line of houses. If you go down some court or alley, as Freeman advises, you see the odd sight of children playing and linen hanging out to dry in little narrow gardens bounded by this immemorial wall. Presently, turning northward, you cross the site of the old east gate, and go along Land Lane, with the wall on one hand and open fields by the Colne on the other. At the north-east corner the wall may be easily climbed. When you reach the top you find that you are on a level with a road within, called Roman Road, planted with trees and

set about with seats. From the wall's summit
you see that the defences of the place were
formerly strengthened with an outer rampart,
the grassy lines of which are still visible towards the river, which perhaps in early times
spread nearer to the town than now. Proceeding
westward through the Castle Park, the wall dis-
appears in some modern mean streets for two or
three hundred yards. Emerging, however, at
North Hill, where another gate formerly stood,
we reach the open space of the cattle market,
and the wall can again be followed ; indeed, it is
quite clear for a long distance westward and
southward up the steep ascent of Balkan Hill.
At the top of this hill there stands what is — with
the sole exception of the one at Lincoln — the
only Roman entrance to a town now left in
England. The Balkan Gate, as it is called, is
almost entirely built of Roman brick. It has a
central round arch eleven feet wide, and two
smaller side entrances protected by a semi-circular
bastion, within which are two guard-rooms. It is
probably to the accidental diversion of the main
stream of traffic from this entrance to that at Head
Gate that we owe the preservation of a relic of
such extreme interest. " How beautiful, " says
Carlyle, " to see thereby, as through a long vista,
into the remote Time ; to have, as it were, an
actual section of almost the earliest Past brought
safe into the Present, and set before your eyes ! "

From this point back to our starting-place, the wall can be followed better from above than from beneath. Sir Isaac's Walk and Eld Lane, which run just within it on the south of the town, are on a level with its top, and many houses actually rest upon it. At two places — one near the church of St Mary-at-the-Wall, where Morant the Essex historian was formerly rector, and the other at Shere-gate near Eld Lane, are traces of former postern-gates ; at each point there is a curious opening in the wall, with steps leading down from within to the level of the outer street.

History tells us little of the condition of the Colony after the fearful events of the revolt and its suppression and allows us to think that between the conquerors and the conquered a milder feeling at last prevailed. At least we are prevented from thinking of the Romans in Britain as mere creatures of avarice and cruelty, by the touching inscriptions which have been found on their tombs in the cemetery that lined the road between Colchester and Lexden. Two priceless relics, now in the museum, appear to me to express most powerfully the double aspect of the Roman character. One, known as the Colchester Sphinx, is a stone figure with a woman's head and the body and breasts of a lioness, with claws fixed in a prostrate human form. The other is a sculptured tombstone, the inscription on which has been translated thus : " Marcus Favonius, son of

Marcus of the tribe of Pollia, the gentle centurion of the twentieth legion. Verecundus and Novicius, his freedmen, placed this. Here is the spot. " Above the epitaph, carved in high relief within a round-arched recess, stands the gentle centurion in his habit as he lived, clad in his tunic and holding the short Roman sword in his hand.

The waning of the power of Rome wrought a change in the fortunes of Camulodunum. The legions in Britain were recalled to defend the seat of empire against the barbarian hordes, and the distant province was left henceforth to shift for itself. By the irony of events this luxurious city with its perfect fortifications was next to be occupied by a race that abhorred walled towns. When the Saxons sailed up the estuary of the Colne, where there was now no longer a Roman fleet to oppose them, they saw the walls of Colonia frowning upon them, and gave the place the name by which it is still known. There can be little doubt that it was from the river that this name was taken — *Colne-ceaster*. Names of rivers generally last longer than any other. This derivation is far more probable than that of *Colonia-ceaster*, while that for King Coel is, as we have seen, purely fanciful. The Saxons overran and took possession of the fields and gardens which had been cleared from the midst of morass and forest round the town, and began to live there after their own fashion. It was not until they were beset by another race of marauders, even fiercer than they themselves had been, that they learned to prize the shelter of the walls which they formerly scorned to dwell in. Early in the tenth century the Danes had seized the town while King Edward the Elder was at Maldon, as we learn from the Anglo-Saxon Chronicle, which tells us : " There gathered mickle folk on harvest, either of Kent and of Surrey and of East-Saxons, and each of the nighest boroughs, and fared to Colchester, and beset the borough all round and there fought till they had won it and the folk all slew, and took all that there within was, but the men that were there fled over the wall. . . . Ilk year afore Martinmas fared Edward King with West Saxons' fyrd (militia) to Colne-ceaster, and repaired the borough and made it new there where it to-broken was. " Perhaps in some of the places where the regularly-built Roman wall has been roughly patched, we have traces of the rude Saxon handiwork.   In Colchester, as elsewhere, little of their actual building remains, since most of their structures were of wood. Still it was probably not more than a century after the wall-repairing by Edward the Elder that the existing tower of Trinity church was built. Large quantities of Roman brick were used in its construction, especially in that of its most striking feature, the tri-angular-headed west doorway. The Saxon genius is unmistakably stamped upon the names of the streets and parishes. The best instance of this is the Hythe, which is pure Anglo-Saxon for a port, and still denotes that part of the town that slopes down to the wharves on the river, while the bold hill that dominates it on the opposite bank is still appropriately termed Greenstead.

With the Norman conquest a new race of great builders and military architects came into possession of the town. The castle built by Eudo de Rie, the dapifer, or steward of William Rufus, has in its walls, curiously enough, a large quantity of Roman brick disposed in the Roman manner, which has led many to attribute to the earlier race a building founded centuries after them. Its keep is the largest remaining in England, larger even than the White Tower of London, which it so resembles in plan that both have been ascribed to one architect, bishop Gundulf of Rochester, with whom Eudo was on friendly terms. As it now stands, the building has lost two storeys of its former height, and of its internal arrangements far less remains than at the neighbouring Castle of Hedingham. Only to the faithful labour of the builders do we owe it to-day that a single stone is left upon another ; for, after the Civil War, it was sold to a private person, who with much effort demolished large portions of it for building-material, and only desisted on finding that the results did not pay for the trouble.

About twenty years after the building of the castle, Eudo Dapifer, who seems to have been pious after the usual manner of Norman lords, founded near it a religious house. The miraculous element in the story is given in the Chronicle compiled by the monks : " Near the city, on the south side of it, there was a little mound on whose northern slope Sigeric, a priest, had a habitation and a church, constructed of wooden planks, dedicated to Saint John the Evangelist. In this church, in the darkness of the night, divine lights were often seen to flash, and voices were heard praising God, while no one was within. It happened also that on the festival of St John a certain man, who was fettered by the King's command and was maintained by the citizens in turn, was present there with many others at the celebration of mass, when suddenly the bolt of his manacles sprang out beyond four or five of the bystanders, and the fetters broke with a noise, and the man stood free, and the whole city rejoiced at the miracle. " On the site of this wooden church, and on the basis of this unquestioning faith, the famous abbey of St John was built by Eudo. He gave great gifts to it, and when he died in Normandy in 1120 his body was brought back by his own desire and buried in the western porch. Fronting a little hilly green, where fairs were formerly held, stands a fine flint gateway of Perpendicular date, all that now remains of the abbey, the rest of whose story will be told presently. Not a trace of the Norman building is left.

56　The Spell of Colchester

It is otherwise with another famous monastic establishment of the town. Just outside the walls, near where St Botolph's gate formerly stood, is a green enclosure beset with trees amid which some imposing but roofless ruins stand. Immense round columns of rubble and flint support wide arches, above which runs another bold arcade. This is the skeleton of the nave. Of the sadly damaged western front enough is still left to show the boldness and harmony of its design. A deeply-recessed central doorway, two arcades of intersecting round arches one above another, a circular window in the angle of the gable, and two flanking towers — such are the main features. Very interesting is the way in which Roman brick has been employed, especially in the arcades, which are wholly composed of them. This is a very unusual and highly decorative arrangement. The priory of St Botolph was founded about 1100 A.D. for Augustine canons, and the Pope gave it precedence over all other English houses of the same order. The splendid priory church was the principal church in Colchester until the siege in 1648. The ruin that we see is all that was left of it by the parliamentary cannon.

Two pictures of Colchester in mediæval times now come under our notice : one of a memorable visit of the court, the other of the daily life of the citizens.

" In May 1157, " says Mr George Rickword, " Colchester witnessed scenes never paralleled in her history. From May 23rd to 28th Henry the Second with his court and the whole machinery of government stayed in the town. Whether accompanied by Queen Eleanor or not, he doubtless occupied his own royal residence, for the Abbey would have its guest-chambers filled with the great ecclesiastics, their chaplains, crossbearers, and serving men, while the royal retinue would have to put up with the poor thatched and timbered cottages of the burghers, and the host of men-at-arms, minstrels, jugglers, light-o'-loves and beggars, probably camped out in the fields round the walls. " Writing of a period a century or two later, Dr Cutts remarks : " Men lived their life out then without going beyond the walls of the borough, except for an occasional holiday within the liberties ; but within those limits they found strongly-marked varieties of human character ; in the town they found the beautiful and picturesque in architecture, sculpture, painting, costume, the dramatic ceremonies of mediæval worship ; and outside the town, yet without transgressing the liberties of the borough, they found, in contrast with all this, cornland and meadow, unreclaimed forest and wild common, shipping and river and sea."

Now comes the fateful period of the Reformation. The priory falls into the hands of the insatiable Audley. The abbot of St John's stoutly refuses to yield to the King. Contemporary evidence suggests that he was playing for a higher pension but his words have a ring of sincerity : " The King shall never have my house but against my will and against my heart, for I know by my learning he cannot take it of right and of law. " His contention was so far justified that he was overcome by treachery, if the tradition be true the " the magistrates asked him to a feast, and then showed him the warrant and went and hanged him without further ceremony."

The abbey was bought in the reign of Edward the Sixth by his Master of Requests, John Lucas, a descendent of whom comes on the scene in a moment. The town seems to have suffered severely from these troubles. Formerly we read in the municipal records of permission granted to citizens to erect posts in the street to support the vines against their houses, which suggests prosperity ; while after the Reformation the town went much to decay, and we are told that twenty-five houses were taken down in Head Street alone.

A century later, when these dissensions had culminated in civil war, Colchester sustained its famous siege of seventy-six days. After two and a half centuries the damage then wrought is still apparent. St Botolph's magnificent church is in fragments, the tower of St Martin's is half gone and nearly all the other churches have suffered.

St Leonard's at the Hythe was stored with pro-
visions and crowded with terrified people when
bombarded from the neighbouring churchyard on
Greenstead hill.

The town had been seized and held by the
Royalists, although its inhabitants as a whole were
favourable to the Roundheads. The besiegers,
however, hemmed in friends and foes alike, the
sooner to starve the latter into submission. The
Royalist officers surrendered to mercy, and two of
them, Sir Charles Lucas and Sir George Lisle,
were shot. Whether Fairfax was justified in exe-
cuting them we are now unable to decide — that
they died bravely is beyond question. " Sir
Charles Lucas, being placed in position to receive
his fate, said, ' I have often looked death in the
face in the field of battle, and you shall now see I
dare to die. '. . . Sir George Lisle looked at the
file of soldiers who were standing prepared to
execute their bloody office, and, thinking them
placed at too great a distance, desired them to
come nearer to him, on which one of them
answered, ' I'll warrant you, sir, we'll hit you. '
Sir George smilingly replied. ' I have been nearer
to you, friends, when you have missed me. ' " The
place of execution was a green spot of ground on
the north side of the castle, a few paces from the
wall. Upon that spot, according to a later tradition mentioned by Defoe, the grass ever after
refused to grow, though it grew abundantly around.

The place is now marked by an inscribed stone placed there by Dr Laver, the eminent archæologist of Colchester. Lucas and Lisle lie buried in the little church of St Giles. After the Restoration their funeral service was magnificently celebrated, and over their grave was placed a large marble slab which declares that these " most valiant captains . . . for their eminent loyalty to their soverain. . . were . . . in cold bloud barbarously murdered."

From this point the romantic interests begins to fade ; Colchester settles down to its trade returns and annual oyster-feast, and pulls down any ancient monuments without compunction. Musing on these things, I find myself one starless summer night wandering again round the old Roman gate. Overhead rises the ugly modern water-tower. Pushing open a heavy iron gate, I tread amid rank grass to the edge of a reservoir. In the stillness I hear, every few moments, a musical gush of water, driven up at regular intervals by the machinery in the pumping-station below the hill. While Colchester sleeps, this indispensable work goes on. And I think that the old Romans, who built that wall and gate, and traces of whose water-courses have been found beneath this very spot, would not, with their practical spirit, have disdained the power which so admirably supplies the daily wants of their successors.

The spell of a magic Past, carelessly hidden beneath a prosaic Present — this is the spell of Colchester.

VII

Behind the Cliffs

" Where peasants tending upland kine
Scan distant sails and scent the brine. "

EAST of Colchester lies a corner of Essex that
pushes out boldly into the North Sea. The
district is known as the Tendring Hundred, from
the little place called Tendring which stands
exactly in its centre. This village needs now to
be sought for, as it lies away from any main road,
and its relations with the great world go no further
than supplying that world with the necessaries of
life from its unobtrusive farms ; yet it must once
have held a proud position when it gave its
name to the entire district. The names of these
" hundreds " are a thousand years old ; in some
instances — as in the present one — the places from
'which they sprang can still be identified, though
much declined ; in others they are names only.
The interests of the Tendring Hundred — save as
regards a few sea-side towns — are still purely
agricultural, as they were three centuries ago,
when John Norden praised the " great and huge

cheeses wondered at for their massiveness and
thickness" which the district produced.

Over all this quiet land blow the winds from
the North Sea, which beats incessantly upon its
crumbling coast. From Colne Point to the Naze
there rises from levels of marsh and creek a long
line of chalk and boulder cliffs, dotted at intervals
by the low martello-towers, which remind us of
the dread of the French invasion which filled the
popular mind in the early years of last century.
Southward and eastward spreads the limitless
watery horizon, stained by the trailing smoke of
steamships. Along the coast one hears the usual
stories of the devastation wrought by the sea — of
submerged towns whose relics can still be discerned
far out at low tide — of church-bells heard to ring
beneath the waves. Is there not a prebend of
St Paul's whose vanished revenues were derived
from a parish now recorded as " Consumpta per
Mare " ? Now over these treacherous cliffs, where
until lately nothing was to be seen but corn and
poppies, or tough grass whistling in the wind,
stare the cheerless frontages of raw new villas and
hotels. How many of those who spend a holiday
at Clacton-on-Sea, with its air of feverish prosperity, give a thought to the mother village of
Great Clacton ? Yet here may be found a knot
of quaint old houses and inns grouped around a
church, to the south door of which a charming
avenue of limes conducts you. The church is

described as Norman, but though it doubtless dates from that period, it is quite unlike the usual type of small, heavily-decorated village churches of the time, being large and bold in conception, and altogether of a quality for which I can find no other word than Romanesque. Under the shadow of its tower stands a beautiful old gabled building known as Church Farm, well worthy to be beside it.

From Clacton you may take the cliff path or go by the sands along the edge of the water to Walton.. Here a quieter tone prevails, the zenith of the town's prosperity as a watering-place belonging to a past generation ; but it still has that curiously restless air of towns that live by providing amusement for visitors. The pleasantest thing I found in Walton was a glimpse of the creek which runs behind it, with a brown-sailed boat threading its way among the fields inland.

We may pause here a moment to consider a point in Essex nomenclature. The surrounding district is locally called " the Sokens, " and its chief places are Walton-le-Soken, Kirby-le-Soken, Thorpe-le-Soken. The word " soken " seems to have been applied to certain Danish communities who settled here, and, as appears from Domesday Book and other sources, were recognised as enjoying exceptional privileges under feudal law. There is a larger proportion of Danish names here than in any other part of Essex

Turning my back now upon the sea-side towns,
I take once more to the lanes. Just after sunset
I reach the quiet little village of Great Oakley,
and find a welcome at the unpretentious inn
prettily named the *May Bush*. While my evening meal is preparing, I stroll down a rough farm
lane which presently brings me to the verge of a
marshy inlet of the sea known as Horsey Mere.
The desolate scene spreads seawards in the
gathering dusk, in which the screaming sea-birds
are hardly visible as they swoop rapidly overhead ;
and just at the doubtful edge of the water can be
descried the skeleton timbers of a rotting upturned
boat. I shiver, and turn back to seek warmth and
light and companionship.

In the little cosy parlour behind the bar the
landlord and I sit on opposite sides of the fire,
each enjoying the solace of a church-warden pipe.
What a suggestion of almost Oriental luxury com-
bined with artistic simplicity there is in the long
white stem that curves so gracefully from lips to
knee ! Outside, in the large flagged kitchen,
where big wooden settles stand at right angles to
the warm chimney corners, some labourers are
resting after their long day's work. Their voices
reach us now and then in the inner room, and the
landlord tells me curious tales concerning them.
At harvest time there have been complaints as to
the quality of the beer supplied to them by the
farmers ; and a custom has therefore arisen of

Great Oakley — The May Bush.

Great Oakley — The May Bush.

giving to each man a quantity of malt and hops, with which to brew for himself sufficient liquor to last him in reason through the whole time of harvest ; but the temptation is, of course, to drink more freely at the beginning, and thus the labourer is discontented at the end. Still, not one of those men in the adjoining room, calling at the house for a pint of beer, however weary and thirsty himself, will touch it until he has handed it to his neighbour, with the words, " Drink, mate. " Nor, I found, would they accept a draught from me until I had put it to my own lips.

Wakened in the morning by the twittering of sparrows in the thatch that sheltered my dormer window, I arose to a blazing day. Keeping steadily along the loose roads for several miles, I came at noon to the village of Thorpe. The friendly and communicative hostess of the *Maid's Head* fell somewhat silent when I asked her if she could tell me anything of Kitty Canham, but vouchsafed the information that she believed this was a person who was buried in the churchyard, and who had had two husbands. I found the grave, and afterwards learned the whole story. In August 1752 a gentleman in disguise landed in the Colne, bringing with him the embalmed body of a lady. He travelled to Thorpe with this strange burden ; and calling upon the Reverend Alexander Gough, then vicar of the parish, asked him to fulfill the last wish of the dead lady, which

E

was that she should be buried in the churchyard there. The vicar was surprised at so singular a request, but infinitely more astonished when he recognised in the lifeless face the features of his own wife, who had deserted him years before. The new-comer then declared himself to be Lord Dalmeny, who was born and had spent his life in Italy, and had married the lady at Verona under the name of Catherine Canham. Surely a stranger funeral can hardly be imagined that that which these two mourners attended.

In the hot afternoon I came to Elmstead Market. Here was a roadside waste with a wheelwright's picturesque litter of wheels and logs left to season in sun and rain. A small square space of green formed the centre of the village, evidently the site of the ancient market. The village of Elmstead stood a further mile north, and there the greater number of the inhabitants formerly dwelt. It is possible that we have here an illustration of the origin of markets as expounded by Sir Henry Maine and others. Markets seem formerly to have been held on neutral ground between separate and probably hostile village communities ; and in course of time became the nucleus of new and larger settlements. Taking a " horse-path, " which the sign-post informed me led to Ardleigh, and following it along a grassy track with plenty of trees on either hand, I came to Elmstead, a church and farmhouse enclosed within the one rectangular belt of trees, principally elms. The church has a plain round-arched doorway, said to be of Saxon date, and, if so, interesting in connection not only with the general history of the parish, but also with its beautiful Saxon name. No tower or spire surmounts the church, yet its general aspect is very pleasing. Its most prominent feature is a parvise-chamber above the south porch, within which a wooden staircase ascends. A swarm of bees was busy on the sunny south wall just beneath the roof. As I turned towards the farmhouse, a picturesque feminine figure disappeared among the bushes of the kitchen garden. The front door stood wide, and revealed the spacious hall, clearly by far the largest room in the house. The master came himself in his shirt-sleeves and with his vest open, but every inch a man and a gentleman, to direct me over the fields.

The day grew late as I strode away southwards from Elmstead, over the high ground overlooking the estuary of the Colne. Presently I came within sight of the tower of Brightlingsea church which from its hundred feet of height, and its splendid position on a hill overlooking the marshes, forms a conspicuous mark for mariners at sea. This handsome embattled building with its spacious windows and bold massive buttresses stands nearly two miles away from the fishing village from which it takes its name. The long street of Brightlingsea lies close to the water. The haven is crowded with the masts of pleasure yachts and oyster-smacks. I was fortunate enough to obtain cosy quarters at the *Swan*. During the evening I looked into the public room of the inn. It was a large parlour with comfortable Windsor chairs set close together all round the walls, and the room held two or three dozen men drinking and smoking in philosophic contentment. Most of them were masters or mates of vessels in the harbour, but there was also a goodly sprinkling of local tradespeople. There was a good deal of racy talk and merriment of that peculiar flavour one gets among seafaring folk.

In the morning I had myself rowed up the creek to the ancient village of St Osyth. It made a charming picture from the water on its low wooded hill, crowned with the buttressed red brick tower of the church. Landing at the wharf near an old water-mill, and ascending a quaint old street, I reached an open green space. In front were the church and the main street of the village, and on the left a range of Tudor buildings, including a handsome flint and stone gateway, very like that of St John's abbey at Colchester.

Here again the same sordid story of spoliation has to be told. Both Audley and Cromwell desired possession of the priory ; and Cromwell, being the more powerful, obtained it. The correspondence between these two men, which still exists, throws a curious light upon the contest.

Audley tries every artifice to gain his end — cajolery, bribery, depreciation of the thing coveted. " Both these houses be in the ends of the shire of Essex. . . . St John lacketh water, and St Osyes standeth in the marshes, not very wholesome, so that few of reputation as I think will keep continual house in any of them. " But Cromwell was obdurate, and kept St Osyth for himself. Yet his enjoyment of this and his other monastic manors in Essex was short-lived ; for by promoting the marriage with Ann of Cleves, he incurred the royal displeasure, and, as Froude observes, he fell like lightning while on the very pinnacle of power. He was beheaded on Tower Hill exactly one year after the surrender of the priory.

Like any other member of an appreciative public I paid my sixpence for permission to view the remains of this famous establishment. The gardens and conservatories, to which my attention was chiefly drawn, were certainly beautiful, but obviously part of a wealthy private mansion. The ascent of an octagonal turret called the Abbot's Tower gave a fine view over the marshes and out to sea. A beautiful Early English chamber now used as a private chapel could be inspected through a grating, but beyond this there was nothing older than the Perpendicular age. As yet I had seen nothing which directly recalled the origin of all this magnificence — the legend of St Osyth. It is a specially interesting one, as showing the

peculiar sanctity attached to the state of virginity
in early Christian times.   In those days of the
Heptarchy, Ositha, or Osyth, was the daughter
of Redwald, the first Christian King of the East
Angles, by Wilburga, daughter of Penda, King of
the Mercians.   In youth she vowed perpetual
virginity, but was betrothed against her will to
Sighere, King of the East Saxons.   Before the
marriage took place, or, as some have it, during the
bridal feast, she stole away and took the veil.
Afterwards she obtained   from Sighere, not only
his consent to relinquish her, but the gift of the
village of Chich in the Tendring Hundred (now
St Osyth) to maintain a nunnery.   She was abbess
here until A.D. 653, when the Danes under
Ingwar and Ubba sacked the convent and beheaded
her.   So much may be sober history, but now
comes the miraculous element inseparable from
the lives of the saints.   she picked up her head,
and, guided by angels, carried it to the church
door, where she knocked and fell prostrate.   At
the spot where she was beheaded, a fountain
gushed out, long renowned for its marvellous
curative virtues.   The monks enclosed it in a
monument and conducted the water through a
leaden pipe, which remained until a modern yachts-
man tore it up for ballast.   Local tradition says
that St Osyth, head in hand, still visits the well
and the church, a white, ghostly figure, scaring
travellers in the Nun's Wood.

When I asked a servant at the priory to be allowed to see the Nun's Wood and the Wishing Well, the request was refused civilly enough, with the formula — twice or thrice repeated — " That part is quite private ; it is closed to the public. " Still, by going round another way, I managed to see the spot — and much besides which I had not looked for, such as the ponds in the wood with their wealth of water-lilies, and the heron's nest, and the lair of the fox beneath the roots of a giant tree, strewn with bones and the carcasses of rooks. The wood lies at the further end of the park, which is some two or three hundred acres in extent. The Wishing Well is a pool, now bricked round. Close by is another spring, perhaps rising from the same source, whose water is deliciously clear and cold. The trees stretch down to the edge of the creek up which the boats of the Vikings came. The look of the place helps one to realise the story, and to recognise that an actual occurrence underlies it. I was glad that I found the spot, all the more so, perhaps, because it was not included in the regular programme for visitors to the priory. When I retired to my chamber at the *Red Lion* that night, I did not fail to remember that in old days " when they went to bed, they did rake up the fire and make a + in the ashes, and pray to God and St Syth to deliver them from fire and from water and from all misadventure. "

VIII

Mersea Island

" A sense of distance—that sense without which there can be no romance. "– *Theodore Watts-Dunton*.

" MERSEA Island ! Where on earth is Mersea Island ? I never heard of it. " Such were the almost invariable exclamations that greeted me when I told people that I intended taking my family thither for a holiday. But if its name is strange to many, the place itself must be strange to many more. Its unsophisticated character may be judged from the fact that when two artist-friends of mine arrived there on foot one Sunday morning, carrying a huge double easel, this apparatus was the subject of much searching of hearts, and was currently reported to be the advanced guard of an expected circus.

The first person to whom I confided my curiosity on the subject of Mersea Island was a commercial traveller whom I met at at the *Swan* at Brightlingsea, and who insisted on driving me all over the Tendring Hundred in his trap the next day. His horror at the mere mention of the place was highly diverting. He had been there once in pursuit of

72

business, and had lost a whole day in consequence, as the tide had risen while he was on the island, and until it had fallen again he could not get off. Naturally, his well meant warnings had no effect on me, as an uncommercial traveller, save to whet the edge of expectation.

Mersea is interesting, first of all, because it is an island. The philosophy of this is admirably expressed in Philip Hamerton's book on *Paris*. " It is wonderful, " he says, " how much the interest of a piece of land is augmented by the simple fact of its being surrounded with water. The reason probably is that the isolation of the land gives it unity and limits, which are the first conditions necessary to any work in the fine arts. Our own faculties are so limited than the infinite always disconcerts them ; but give us something so defined that we can see its boundaries, and we have the comfortable sensation that perhaps we may understand what lies within them. This feeling about islands is naturally in inverse ratio to their size. . . . The perfection of an island is to be just big enough for some variety of hill and dale, and yet so little that the whole circumference of it can be seen from some elevated point. " The whole of this description applies beautifully to Mersea, which is five miles long by two broad, hilly and much diversified. But it is interesting in many other ways, as I hope to show.

Mersea is best approached from Colchester.

Close to the ancient priory of St Botolph, then, we found in the yard of an inn a medley collection of carriers' carts, one of which bore the name of *Rudlin, West Mersea, SX.* As soon as we beheld this vehicle, we felt that our holiday had really begun. It resembled more than anything else a big gipsy van, and was laden inside and out with baskets, barrels, boxes, and packages of all kinds. A long roomy seat, intended for the accommodation of human beings, ran round the interior, which was lighted by the opening in the front, and by a little practicable window at the back. The proprietor was a short ruddy-faced man with spectacles and a humorous twinkle : we took a liking to him at once, and also to his wife, who sat in a corner, amidst all the chaos, quietly knitting. They readily agreed to take us to Mersea and to find us a lodging there. Presently the horses were harnessed in, and the lumbering vehicle got into motion. A twelve miles' drive was before us. Having somehow imagined that the country between Colchester and the coast would be bare and uninteresting, we were agreeably surprised to find ourselves going along a winding road, full of gentle ups and downs, and bordered nearly all the way by overhanging trees. The evening wind that met us as we rode along smelt more and more of the sea. We were travelling along the track of the celebrated earthquake of 1884, that wrought so much damage not only

in Colchester, but in the villages lying to the south
of it. At Peldon, where we stayed for refreshment at the *Rose*, the church tower had suffered
severely. Just after leaving Peldon, we got our
first glimpse of Mersea Island — a long wooded hill
beyond a gleam of water. Presently we saw that
the island was connected with the mainland by a
long causeway, marked out on each side by a row
of white stakes; and soon we were crossing this
causeway with the water lapping the stones on
each side of us. The Strood, as this narrow strip
of land is called, was formerly only visible at low
water ; but it has since been raised, and is now
passable at all ordinary states of the tide. It was
originally laid down (like so much else of practical
utility) by the Romans, who seem to have gone to
Mersea for oysters, and, perhaps also for pleasure.
It is said, at least, that West Mersea village church
(whose massive square tower now comes into view)
stands on the site of a temple to Vesta. Centuries
afterwards, we find Mersea a stronghold of the
Danes. Hastings, a great man among them about
the end of the ninth century, made it his headquarters, and tried to found a sort of petty kingdom
'here. It was here that Alfred ran the invaders
to earth. In times quite near to our own it was a
notorious haunt of smugglers.

The village of West Mersea stands amid trees
and cornfields overlooking its chief means of liveli-
hood — the oyster-smacks moored below. As we

took up our abode here with a family of fisher-folk, we had a good opportunity of studying the oyster-dredging industry. One day the " boys " having offered to show me the whole art and mystery of their calling, I rose by arrangement at 4 A.M. The morning was dark and raw, the wind whistled round the house, and ragged-edged slate-coloured clouds scurried across the sky. I hurried into my clothes, swallowed a biscuit and a cup of milk, and followed my stalwart blue-jerseyed companions down to the "Hard," as the firm shingle path is called which runs down to low-water mark. From thence we rowed out to the *Vesta*, a little craft of eleven tons. A good deal had to be done in arranging the gear for the day's work, so I had ample time to look about me in the keen morning air. After a while a stream of smoke began to arise from the cabin chimney, accompanied by a savoury odour. Presently we all descended to the cabin, a smoky little den just roomy enough to sit up in. Breakfast was welcome indeed, and the primitive cuisine merely completed the *tout ensemble.*

Oyster-dredging is hard work. I never saw men work harder than those men did for the next six or seven hours. Steering the smack into the open sea and letting her drift, they throw out a number of drag-nets made of iron and strong ox-hide, and pull them up again full of *cultch* — that is, oyster-shells, stones, and miscellaneous rubbish, to which the spat or spawn of the oyster attaches itself.

Quickly emptying the net upon the deck and flinging it back into the water, they dexterously sort out the cultch with a species of blunt knife. The mere rubbish is thrown overboard again, while the young oysters are separated and put back into the river to mature. Part of the work of the dredgers consists in searching for any of the natural enemies of the oyster, such as the starfish, mussel, or whelk-tingle, and taking care that none of these are returned to the water. It is a curious fact that oysters have their good and bad seasons, according to the weather, like corn, and cannot develop without a sufficiency of sunshine. Their cultivation has been carried on in these islands since the dawn of our history. Dr Laver reminds us that "in no instance is any excavation made about the Roman stations of this kingdom without oyster shells being found in abundance; and even in Rome itself, shells are found bearing the peculiar characters of a Colne oyster." Returning to our own times, a few years ago, some oyster fishers belonging to Tollesbury, on the Blackwater, having taken cultch from the river Crouch, and a dispute ensuing between them and the Burnham men, some of the latter boarded a Tollesbury boat and threw the cultch back into the river. The newspapers reported this incident under the startling title "Piracy in the Crouch."

The drag-nets used in dredging will not act well unless a strong breeze be blowing, therefore the boat pitches violently all the time; it has a steeply curving deck, but no bulwarks, and the men seem likely every moment to be precipitated into the sea; yet they keep their footing without the slightest apparent effort. Work being over early in the afternoon, we run for home before a fresh breeze. The long arm of the rudder has been swinging about all day like the hand of a compass, a few inches above the level of the deck. Lying at full length, resting upon his elbow, the eldest boy leans his shoulder against the tiller, and scanning the sea ahead of him, he steers the vessel by simply increasing or relaxing the pressure.

East Mersea at the opposite end of the island, may be reached by several ways, from any of which a good idea may be obtained of inland Mersea with its harmonious contrasts of form and colour in long-roofed farmsteads amidst their trees and cornfields and distant glimpses of the sea. The village of East Mersea consists of a few scattered cottages with a picturesque ivied church. A former rector here was Mr S. Baring. Gould, whose powerful story *Mehalah* embodies the wilder spirit of Mersea life and scenery. Facing East Mersea lies Brightlingsea, crowded with the masts of its fishing fleet; the channel between is gay with yachts. Returning to the western end of the isle by the shore, one finds delightful little grassy shaded nooks close to the water's edge, with here and there a beach of firm clean sand. To those who seek an orthodox seaside holiday, however, especially with children, Mersea cannot be recommended. Its charm is not of the bucket-and-spade variety.

On the other side of West Mersea spread the marshes, protected from the inroads of the tide by the sea-wall, a raised bank of stones and earth about eight feet high, forming a rude path which follows all the tortuous windings of the shore. Not only on this island, but everywhere around the coast of Essex, except where for some miles they are guarded by low crumbling cliffs, this wall extends. History seems silent on the question to what age we owe this characteristic feature of the district which Morris graphically terms

" The doubtful place
  Where the sea sucks the pasture's blood. "

As you proceed, all houses are left behind, and you see nothing but the water and the muddy foreshore on the one hand, and the wide-stretching pastures on the other, where here and there a few cattle are feeding. The only sounds that break the stillness are the hoarse melancholy cries of the sea-birds and the low rustle of the sedges in the dykes. As twilight approaches, the expanse seems to grow vaster, and the desolate scene has a wonderful weird beauty. Having often wandered for miles amid such surroundings, I cannot imagine it possible to feel more absolutely *alone*. To be really cast adrift in such a place, one feels, would be awful ;

and it is just this, perhaps, that gives it its peculiar fascination. It is well for us sometimes to be disconcerted by the infinite, and to feel our insignificance amid the immensity of the earth, the sea, and the sky.

Osea Island — The Causeway.

Hill Farm, near Stebbing — Agricultural Cart Shed.

IX

Concerning Carriers' Carts

" A respectable, if somewhat lumbering, class of conveyance, much resorted to by decent travellers not overstocked with money."—*Thomas Hardy : Some Crusted Characters.*

THE mention of carriers' carts in the last chapter argues an occasional lapse from those strict principles of Pedestrianism in which I have carefully brought myself up. Those to whom such lapses must of necessity be allowed should try this humble mode of conveyance.

Go into an inn-yard in any of our old country towns during the middle of the day, and you are almost sure to come upon one or more of them ; or if you take up the local almanack, you will find a list giving the names of the carriers, the villages they come from, and their times of coming and going. The names of the owners painted on the sides of the vehicles are names that smack of the soil. The names of the villages they come from you have most likely never heard of. If you have seen the names before, they conveyed no idea to your mind ; you did not actually realise that these places existed. The cart with its owner's name and address upon it gives you something concrete. Jacob in the story was sceptical as to his son having sent for him out of a far country : but " when he saw the waggons, his spirit revived, and he said, 'It is enough.'"

To go " by the carrier, " as the country folk call it, is a sure way to see some unsophisticated people and places.   Formerly there were carriers everywhere ; now they are only found in places remote from the railway.   Their business is to fetch and carry merchandise to and fro between the villages and the market towns.   Incidentally they accommodate the humbler sort of people.   The carrier always lives in a village.   He usually starts early in the morning, arrives in the town about midday, and returns during the afternoon.   Those who have a specially long distance to travel often go one day and return the next.   It would be easy to go over a large part of England, especially in the eastern counties, without any fixed itinerary, but with the certainty of seeing much that is characteristic, by simply changing from one carrier to another in the different villages or towns to which they might happen to take you.

The system is a survival of the rough and ready ways by which in earlier times practical needs were met, and met on the whole very comfortably.   There is nothing cut-and-dried or machine-made about it.   Thus of the vehicles employed hardly two are alike.   The villager

who sets up in business as a carrier does so
with the best vehicle he can afford : if his
business prosper, he has better ones built to
his own design. It may fall to your lot to ride
in a large open cart, a waggonette, a covered
van, or a sort of private omnibus. You are
always liable to be incommoded by the boxes,
bales, or barrels, which it is the carrier's primary
duty to deliver. Carriers take life in a leisurely
fashion, like most country people. The times at
which they are supposed to start may be taken
as approximate. You need not fear being left
behind if you do not arrive to the minute,
especially if you have told the carrier before-
hand that you are coming. If anyone whom
the carrier expects does not come at the proper
time, the carrier will cheerfully wait half-an-hour
or more. He seems to feel no annoyance at
being kept waiting, but much solicitude for the
welfare of the loiterer. This sort of thing is
only possible in the real country. When at
length the horses have been harnessed, and everything arranged in readiness for a start, the carrier,
after seeing that all his fellow-travellers are as
comfortable as circumstances will permit, mounts
to his seat, takes the reins, and with a flourish
of his whip drives through the archway into
the gabled street. In a very short while the
town comes to an end, giving place to fields on
either hand and leafy boughs overhead. Every

now and then a halt is made at a cottage, or at some stile with a house a field or two behind it, and sundry parcels are exchanged with much leisurely discourse in the broad local dialect. It is really wonderful what complicated messages these carriers manage to remember, and what a variety of commissions they execute in the towns for the isolated country people. This fact was remarked by a clergyman newly come into an Essex parish, who complimented the local carrier upon his powers of mind. " Yes," replied the carrier, in perfect good faith, " if you had my job, you would have to wake up. "

Carriers are most useful acquaintances. They know the country and the people — none better — and can often tell you just what you want to know. In the course of the drive of an hour or two they can form some notion of your object in traversing the country, and can tell you accurately the reputation and capabilities of the different inns. In their company you quickly learn what the people of the district are doing and thinking, They are nearly always cheerful and communicative, and usually themselves full of character. I have ridden with many of them, and hope to ride with many more.

One carrier I remember looking pityingly at the occupants of a motor-car which was standing in the High Street of an Essex market-town. He would not care to ride in a horseless carriage, he confided to me, because " there would be nothing to look

at ." Another was a connoisseur in liquid refreshment. Stopping on the way to Chelmsford at a
pretty low-raftered inn where the ale was said to
be exceptionally fine, he pointed out to me the advantage of drinking it drawn fresh from the wood,
instead of after it had passed through metal pipes.
resuming his seat, he talked about his home-made
wines, described the process of manufacture, esti-
mated the quantity in his cellar, and grew eloquent
over the virtues and flavour of each separate vint-
age. Every time that he added a fresh piece of information, he turned round, with a broad smile
that showed the whitest of teeth, nodded his head
with emphasis, and solemnly winked in a way that
was indescribably comic.

I went with a carrier once who struck me as
having more than these men usually possess of
shrewd insight into common every-day things.
Some remark he made led me to quote a text
of Scripture. He looked round at me like a
war-horse that hears the trumpet, and preached
there and then a discourse on my text that for
sheer practical wisdom and terseness of expression
was in its way a masterpiece. I found afterwards
that this man was a leading member of the Peculiar
People, which perhaps explains the marked acer-
bity of language which occurred when his cart
nearly collided with the trap of the village doctor.

By way of contrast, another carrier, whose cart
bore a Christian name surely never before printed

outside the pages of the Bible, was extraordinarily taciturn. My family were with me, and we could hardly get a word out of him beyond Yes and No. This was a little disconcerting, as we were rather dependent on his good offices in finding suitable quarters for us in the remote village to which we were bound. When we got to the end of our journey, and alighted in the yard of an inn, he handed us over without ceremony to his widowed sister, who kept it. From that moment we were surrounded with an atmosphere of almost af- fectionate kindness, so that, with the happiest memories of Essex hostelries, I can hardly recall the like.

X

Along the Stour

" A distant dearness in the hill,
A secret sweetness in the stream." —*Tennyson*.

THE strong tides of the North Sea race round the promontory that forms the north-east extremity of Essex. This promontory juts boldly northward, where the Stour debouches into the ocean, as if to bar its further passage, and points directly up into the mouth of the Orwell. Of the latter river, the left bank curves sharply round below Felixstow, and continues southward to Landguard Point, thus almost completely enclosing the projecting corner of Essex. The town of Harwich, built upon this sheltered tongue of land, forms as it were the pivot on which the flowing and the ebbing tides revolve. The confluence of the widening Stour and Orwell at this point makes of their joint estuary a considerable body of salt water, which, thanks to the opposing curves of the two counties on either hand, forms a magnificent natural harbour. Hence upon its wide expanse of rippling and glittering water, bounded by low green shores and sandy spits, may always be seen a goodly fleet of white-

87

sailed yachts and of humbler fishing-craft. The
ancient town of Harwich lifts its church towers
and lighthouses in the midst, but has seen its
best days, in spite of its natural and historic importance as a seaport. It has been so far rebuilt
as to have lost much of the quaintness it must
have formerly possessed, while such improvements
as have been made since the early Victorian age
have been chiefly in laying out the formal cliff
walk in a southerly direction towards Dovercourt.
If you are arriving from the Continent, the steamer
passes close to the battered pier, the massive
timbers of which are covered with sea-weed and
green slime ;   leaning over the rail are the usual
groups of sight-seers, and the hotel rises above
it with the faded majesty of a generation ago.
The vessel does not pause here but passes
further up the estuary into the new anchorage
at Parkeston.

If from this point we desire to see the country
from the best point of view — that of the leisurely
pedestrian — we shall find a good road leading westward, skirting the southern bank of the Stour. The
eye is charmed by the noble width of the estuary,
beyond which the Suffolk fields slope upwards to
the wooded heights that on the other side overlook
the Orwell. If the tide be at the flood, and the
Stour estuary be full of water, the prospect is indeed
a beautiful one ;   while at the ebb, when a narrow
ribbon of water is seen making its way between

wide flat banks of mud, which contrast finely with
the tillage and pasture above high-water mark, it
is hardly less beautiful. Our road runs close to
the shore; and on the left hand are rich fields
and woods. Whatever be the meaning of the old saying " Near trees, no corn, " it is certainly
disregarded here. When I passed this way the
reapers were busily getting in an opulent harvest,
and the strong light beating upon the yellow
wheatfields was relieved by dark masses of shadow
thrown by giant elms and oaks with which the
fields were surrounded. Presently the little village
of Bradfield came in sight, one of the type that
never fails to charm, with the square stone church
tower rising above the red roofs of the houses
that clustered closely around it. The road, now
skirting an undulating park, approaches the water
again, and brings me into the little town of Mistley.
This is as far as the sea-going ships can come up the
estuary ; for beyond this point there is not
enough water to float vessels of more than a
hundred tons ; so we find a number of them
anchored at the quay, unloading coal or loading
hay and corn. A little further is the railway
junction at Manningtree, from which the line to
Harwich takes a wide sweep. Here the estuary
terminates in a vast stretch of waste land, which
when I saw it in the late afternoon at low tide,
was impressive with the melancholy of treacherous
green marsh and oozy mud dotted with pools and

intersected with trickling streams. Fringed by this debatable land are rich meadows on which herds of cattle are feeding, and which have always, I suppose, been good pasture, as Shakespeare speaks with such peculiar relish of a "roasted Manningtree ox."

Above Manningtree the scenery of the Stour valley changes completely. Untroubled by the tides of the sea, the river flows down peacefully between clearly-defined banks, where the cattle are mirrored as they drink of its waters, and turns the wheels of immemorial water-mills. On the road that skirted the shore of the estuary, the river was the dominant feature of the landscape ; here, although its presence is always made known, it is mainly by endless subtle suggestions, and you only occasionally meet it face to face.

On the evening of that bright summer day of which I have spoken, I was making for Dedham, where I wished to sleep. The sun had set before I left the marshes of Manningtree behind me ; and as I followed a path through the meadows near Lawford, the forms of the horses and cattle feeding by the river were already indistinct, and the distant woodlands growing shadowy with twilight. The path at length led upward, and became a narrow track between the rustling wheat that stood shoulder-high on either hand. As I reached the brow of the slight hill, I saw the large round harvest-moon glowing through the warm haze, and in the light of it a square church-tower. At the end of the field was a stile ; and getting over it I found myself, with surprise, standing in the silent street of Dedham. At the *Marlborough Head* the mere mention of the *May Bush* at Oakley was enough to ensure a welcome. The room in which I was bidden to make myself at home had a curiously carved beam running diagonally across the ceiling, and it is supposed that this part of the house was open on two sides to the street, and supported at the angle by a wooden pillar. It stands just opposite the church, and may have been used for the transaction of business in the days when Dedham was a flourishing seat of the weaving trade. Many of the old clothiers' houses still remain, and are of great interest, together with several ancient inns, and the grammar-school and almshouses for decayed tradespeople, founded by one William Littlebury in 1571. The church itself bears witness to the history of the place, having been built not by some territorial lord, but by two woollen manufacturers named Webbe, father and son, whose merchant's marks appear on the tower, together with the red and the white rose, the badge of Henry the Seventh, then reigning.

But the chief interest of Dedham lies for most people in the fact that it is the gate, so to speak, of that beautiful country which has been made

famous by the genius of Constable. The well-
known picture of the Vale of Dedham was painted
from the summit of the church tower at Langham,
some three miles further west; and there is hardly
a phase of the scenery of this beautiful river valley
in any of its aspects of sky or season which Constable has not seized for us. This man, a miller's
son, gifted not only with artistic perceptions and
powers, but also with a rare appreciation of classic
styles and the environment — so different from his
own — from which these sprang, could yet find
nothing in the world more beautiful than the
scenes of his boyhood, which, as he said himself,
made him a painter. The loving faithfulness with
which he depicted them was well expressed in
the saying of his brother, who knew a good deal
about machinery if but little about painting, that
" John's mill-wheels looked as if they would go
round. " A native of Essex, of course, he was
not ; but it is Essex as well as Suffolk that he
paints, and that in the following passage he describes: " The beauty of the surrounding scenery,
its gentle declivities, its luxuriant meadow flats
sprinkled with flocks and herds, its well-cultivated
uplands, its woods and rivers, with numerous scattered villages and churches, farms and picturesque
cottages, all impart to this particular spot an
elegance hardly anywhere else to be found. "
Elsewhere he says that " nothing can exceed the
beautiful appearance of the country, its freshness,

its amenity." Here Constable shows, I think, that
he can use the pen as well as the brush ; but
there is another remark of his, referring to Stoke
Church, which exactly expresses a peculiarity of
English landscape that I do not remember to have
been pointed out before: " The length of the nave,
with its continuous line of embattled parapet, and
its finely-proportioned chancel, may challenge the
admiration of the architect, as well as its majestic
tower, which from its commanding height may be
said to impart a portion of its own dignity to the
surrounding country. "

The windings of the Stour may be followed on
foot for many miles along the tow-path, or with
a rowing-boat it is paradise in ideal weather.
Barges still ply as far up as Sudbury. It is
much to be regretted on many grounds that
canals and navigable rivers have — largely owing
to the railway monopoly — fallen so much into
disuse among us. Only the most hardened Phil-
istine can fail to see the beauty of carrying heavy
merchandise to remote places where it will be
useful, in a perfectly easy and noiseless manner
through the very heart of green England. The
readiness with which these seemingly unwieldy
craft answer to the slightest touch of the helm
or to the pull of a rope, the light ripples they
raise as they glide through the water, the skill
of the bargemen, throwing the rope into waves
to bring it clear of the bushes, the patience and

intelligence of the horses, — it is the sight of such things that make a real holiday. Well do I remember how one summer day I hailed a barge-man on the Stour, and struck a friendly bargain with him, in virtue of which I spent the rest of the day upon his foremost vessel (there was a string of three), seated upon the sun-warmed tarpaulin, or walking about, as the fancy took me. We travelled at a speed of certainly not more than three miles an hour through luscious meadows brilliant with buttercups, and the softest and greenest of midsummer foliage. Every few miles a tower or spire would come into view, which after leisurely windings at length would be reached ; here would be found a bridge, and perhaps a water-mill and a lock. The process of getting the barges one at a time through the locks was complicated and slow. On these unfrequented rivers, where every bend in the stream is a fresh vision of beauty, and where nothing intervenes to break the spell, one is admitted indeed into real intimacy with our lovely land. The rest to soul and body is complete. But after a while the very *dolce far niente* becomes a cloying sweetness: one tires of inactivity, and longs to tread the earth again.

Along the Stour are many sequestered villages more or less worthy of note, with churches of interest and antiquity. No one should fail to see the little Norman building at Boxted, the massive

round tower of Lamarsh, or the Norman tower at
Mount Bures. Close by the church at the latter
place is the mound from which it takes its distinc-
tive name — a moated stronghold some eighty
feet high. There are many such moated mounds
scattered about the county, but their origin is
by no means clear ; some learned men regard
them as the remains of fortresses hastily thrown
up by the Normans on their arrival, to secure
them against a hostile population ; others are
disposed to attribute them to the Danes or even
to the early Celtic tribes of Britain. Be this as
it may, they are indubitably ancient, and always
give a special charm to the localities in which they
are found.

The Stour in its course runs close to the source
of another Essex river, the Colne, which rises in
the parish of Stambourne, of which the reader
has possibly never heard. "Let him," to quote the
words of one who has spent his boyhood in the place,
"mentally put together certain up and down roads,
with broad margins of green walls of hedge:
ponds, with ducks and goslings, *ad lib.* ; plots of
woodland ; fields of turnips, oats and barley ; a
windmill ; two or three nice houses, with gardens
and lawns ; numbers of cottages which could
hardly be less picturesque ; great wealth of fine
trees ; stretches of meadow land ; valleys and
undulations ; pigs and donkeys ; and withal, a
general disorderliness of fertility, and a sense of

being out of the world, and having nothing particular to do, and you are getting an idea of Stambourne. " This description is by an author whose fame is not usually associated with topography — the celebrated Spurgeon. Whatever may be thought of his theology, or of his method of presenting it, Spurgeon evidently inherited from his sturdy Essex stock two qualities that are humanly appreciable — his broad racy humour and a love for his native fields.

Now that we have turned our backs upon the Stour, let us go a little further and visit Castle Hedingham. This place is so full of architectural and historic interest that I cannot hope here to do justice to it ; nor is the attempt needed. Let me briefly record my first impressions.

It is a day in early autumn, and my progress has been much impeded by the blackberries which the hedges hold so temptingly aloft. Night has already fallen before I reach the village. At last, however, the welcome light streams forth from the open door of the *Bell*, where I am accommodated for the night. My chamber is obviously ancient, and very large, stretching apparently across the whole front of the house. Waking early, I see the gilded sign just outside my window, and look out on the village street. What a sight now greets me ! — the noble Castle keep, a great mass of grey stone towering above

Castle Hedingham — The Bell.

Castle Hedingham — The Keep.

the trees, its grim outline somewhat softened by
their foliage and by the morning haze. It is
the ancient home of the De Veres, the famous
earls of Oxford. After breakfast I proceed to
visit the Castle, procuring a ticket of admittance
at a little shop hard by for three prosaic pence.
Beautiful in its sheer severity of form from the
outside, it is far more beautiful within. Climbing a winding staircase, you come at last upon
a marvellous sight—the great banqueting hall.
Of noble dimensions, being those of the inner
walls of the keep, it has one striking feature
which is, I believe, unique — the vast Norman
arch which supports the roof, strretching in one
magnificent sweep from wall to wall. Another
arch similar in design, though of course much
smaller, adorns the immense open fireplace at the
end of the hall, and completes the picture. Around
the apartment, between the narrow windows, are
a number of round-headed doorways, which, when
entered lead to other doorways at right angles,
forming the entrance to sleeping-chambers
hollowed out in the thickness of the wall.
Over the doorways are iron curtain-rods and
staples which, for aught I know, may have been
there since these cell-like chambers were used
for their original purpose. It is said that
Hedingham is the most perfect remaining specimen in England of a Norman keep ; certainly
no other that I have seen has impressed me

so strongly.   Like some great phenomenon of Nature, it is beyond statement and beyond praise ; yet it was built by human hands.   One can only feel proud to belong to the race that built it

XI

Warp and Weft

" Not slothful in business, fervent in spirit."

THE great and mighty family which produced twenty Earls of Oxford, and retained their title and estates in one direct line for nearly six hundred years, was founded by Alberic de Vere, who came into England with the Conqueror. William gave him his half-sister Beatrix in marriage and the manor of Colne. About the year 1100 his son Alberic or Aubrey de Vere built Hedingham Castle, and also, after the fashion of the times, founded a monastery near it. It is said that this second Aubrey de Vere had a son Geoffrey who was recovered from a sickness by the Abbot of Abingdon, who was skilled in physic. Hence Colne Priory, as it came to be called, was subordinated to Abingdon Abbey. It stands — what remains of it — but a few miles south-east from Hedingham, among the pastures through which winds the sluggish Colne ; indeed, so near to the river that the monks are said to have fished from

99

the windows. The buildings were framed of massive oak filled in with bricks laid herring-bone fashion. Part of the Norman wall en-closing the priory gardens is still standing. The priory, suppressed in 1536 with others of the lesser monasteries, was for some reason not granted to one of the typical court favourites, but to a DeVere, the contemporary representa-tive of the founder's family, which had long had a seat in this parish named Hall Place. Nearly fifty years later the seventeenth Earl of Oxford sold it to his steward, Roger Harlakenden, in whose family it has remained ever since. It may therefore be said to have changed hands only once in the whole course of its history ; and curiously enough, Roger Harlakenden, him-self was a direct descendant of William Har-lakenden, who came over at the Conquest as esquire to Alberic de Vere. It may be added that from this same Harlakenden family have sprung two notable representatives of modern literature — Anne Gilchrist and John Addington Symonds.

The priory church has long since disappeared. Morant, writing over a century ago, says that stables were built upon the site. Part of the foundations can still be made out in summer, when the grass becomes parched more quickly there than in the surrounding spaces. The rest of the priory buildings have been converted into the

usual private residence, showing but little trace
of the original structure. Attached to the present
mansion is a sort of cloister, in which are preserved three altar tombs, with recumbent effigies
of earls of Oxford, removed from the priory
church on its demolition. During a rebuilding
of the present priory, these tombs were lent to
the neighbouring parish church ; and their subsequent replacement in their present position
caused considerable stir in the public journals in
June 1884. The church itself, though a fine and
spacious one, strikes the visitor as rather cold and
bare, a feeling which the presence of these monuments would certainly help to remove ; but it is
said that while they reposed there they were considerably embellished by bucolic clasp-knives, and
this may justify the means taken to ensure
their preservation. For beautiful monuments they
certainly are ; the details of feature, costume,
and armour being remarkably interesting, while
the tombs themselves, in freestone, are Decorated
work of great beauty.

"From whatever point we approach the village, "
says Mr Herbert Gilchrist, " we see rising 'mid
elms the church tower, encirled beneath the
battlements with stars picked out in flint. " Yet
it must be confessed — and here we approach the
point of this chapter — that the most prominent
object of the village, or small town, as it should
be called, is not the church-tower, but a tall

chimney. For even the pastoral Colne Valley has here a manufactory for agricultural implements, and a silk-winding factory. And at Halstead, a little town close by that rises picturesquely beyond a bridge over the same quiet river, you will find the long unlovely lines of red brick buildings and artisans' cottages that tell the same tale. There are two weekly newspapers, and not long ago there was actually a " strike " of the girls employed in the silk mills. At Braintree, a characteristic country market-town, you will be astonished to hear the hum of machinery. We ask ourselves, how does the factory system come to take root and flourish in the very heart of rural Essex ?

The answer to this question is instructive. We have seen for example, that Dedham was a flourishing centre of the woollen trade as early as the fourteenth century. Coggeshall — a quaint old place, which boasts the remains of a beautiful Cistercian abbey founded by Stephen and Maud, and refused the railway sixty years ago — was for centuries a rival of Dedham. The art of weaving cloth seems to have been carried on in Essex from very early times, having been introduced by the Romans, before whose arrival the inhabitants clad themselves in fleeces and skins of beasts. For centuries, wool continued to be the basis of clothing. Before the rise of commerce, probably every last village had a weaver in its midst, who simply supplied the needs of its inhabitants.

In the towns, as was natural, the work was carried on upon a rather larger scale, perhaps with the aid of mechanical power, but still mainly for local purposes. But after a time, when the fine breeds of English sheep became famous, and the Low Countries, commercially in advance of us, began to import our fleeces in large quantities, the lords of the soil found out that it was more profitable to grow sheep than corn — a discovery the after-effects of which were so greatly regretted by More and other public-spirited men. The policy of Edward the Third, forbidding the export of English wool, struck a blow at the prosperity of the Netherlands, and helped at the same time to change the face of England. The Flemings flocked hither in large numbers in search of work at their accustomed trade, and received encouragement and protection. Most of them came from Bruges. Landing at Harwich — a port of vastly greater importance then than now — they travelled inland by the good roads leading thence to the centres of the woollen industry in Essex. It is noteworthy that all these towns are situated upon the rivers — such as the Stour, the Pant, the Colne — with which Essex is so well supplied, and from which power to drive the looms could be obtained. The Flemings gave a fresh impetus to the trade, not only by the mere fact of their arrival, but by the introduction of new methods of manufacture. They must also have brought with them, from the self-governing towns which they had quitted, some of their hereditary instinct of independence and freedom. Another and even more important element was introduced a little later. The cruel persecutions inflicted by the Duke of Alva caused many more of the Flemings to leave their homes and settle amidst their compatriots in Essex, encouraged therto by Elizabeth, the sworn foe of the Spaniard. The seed of religious liberty, strengthened by resistance to the power that sought to crush it, was brought hither and planted in a congenial soil. The lives of these people were marked by patient industry and sober earnestness. They were thrifty, and maintained their own poor. Their reputation for honesty was such that the " seals " affixed by them to the bales of their own goods were sufficient warranty of quality and quantity to the buyers, who did not trouble to open the package. A temper which united practical business aptitude with piety verging on mysticism has often manifested itself in the world's history, and always as a powerful force. To this may be attributed the successful undertakings originally founded in these centres by Fleming settlers whose names they still bear. The name of Courtauld, to take one example, is a name to conjure with in the Colne valley. In the same way the well-known Martineau family are descended from Huguenot refugees who settled in Norwich. This leads me to note, further, that the presence of factories

in these Essex valley lands is not the only surprising thing : you also come upon quaint old-
world meeting houses, many of them still used
for worship by the Unitarians, a body not numeri-
cally large, taking the country as a whole, and
recruited mainly from the centres of intellectual
culture. How does this arise ? It would appear
that the Flemings, having themselves shaken off
the yoke of an alien creed, wished to leave their
descendants free from any fetter upon their faith.
Usually the trust-deed of a chapel founded under
their influence is so framed that the building is
dedicated solely " to the worship of God. " This
shows at least that persecution had taught these
people the right lesson, that of tolerance, and not
the evil lesson of counter-persecution.

In the century following that of the second
coming of the Flemings, the same drama re-enacts
itself, but it is now not immigration, but emigra-
tion that we have to witness. How far the
Puritan revolt against ecclesiastical rigidity had
been reinforced by the new foreign element I
am unable to say ; but it is clear that the inhabitants of these Essex towns took no small part
in founding the new England beyond the sea.
We find today an *Essex county* and a *Dedham*
in Massachusetts. The late Colonel Chester, who
had made this subject a special study, wrote :
" My investigations enable me to affirm unhesi-
tatingly that of the early New England settlers

the origin of considerably more than one half can be traced directly or indirectly to the county of Essex. " Here, however, the pious weavers of Essex pass out of our chronicle, since it is on other shores that they continue to weave " the web of human things."

XII

Amidst the Wheat

" How curious! how real!
Underneath the divine soil, overhead the sun."–*Whitman*.

TRAVELLING one day by the Great Eastern Railway, I had to " change " at Witham Junction.
Crossing the bridge, my attention was arrested
by a little village perched upon a hill quite near
to the station ; so I strolled in that direction,
intending to return in half-an-hour in time to
continue my journey. That journey was never
finished, however. On closer inspection my village proved to be quite as charming as it had
appeared at a distance, and I felt that to hurry
away from it would be sinful. I decided to stay
there for the night, and took no thought for the
morrow.

The village consisted of a few score houses and
`cottages, mostly ancient, interspersed with trees,
and grouped upon the sides of the hill around the
church, which occupied the usual place of honour at
the summit. Viewed in any aspect, the place formed
a perfectly harmonious picture. The church itself
is an interesting building in which the beautiful

work of the fourteenth century predominates. Immediately below it is an irregular open green space which at once suggested the idea of a market ;   and I found afterwards that an important market had formerly been held here on Sundays.   Indeed the market gave the little place its name, which is not Witham but Chiping Hill.   The original Witham seems to have stood where Chipping Hill now stands — a fortified place upon the rising ground.   The Saxon Chronicle tells us that in the year 913 " king Edward went with some of his forces to Maeldune (Maldon) in Essex, while the Burg at Witham was wrought. "   In later centuries a new colony sprang up outside the stronghold, and spread itself towards the south.   This is now the pleasant old town of Witham, which has several ancient coaching inns, and is locally known as Newland Street.   Still the people resorted to the hill, to worship at the parish church, and to buy and sell at the market, which (as the word " chipping " suggests) from time immemorial had been held there.   Since the building of the railway, which runs between the two places, they have been separated more sharply than ever ;   and now, happily for the antiquary and lover of the picturesque, Chipping Hill is left pretty much to itself.

Away to the north the country looked inviting, and tempted me to explore it.   It was nearly

harvest :   the corn stood thick in the fields on
either hand, the innumerable heavy ears, each
proudly balanced on its slender stalk, presenting
in the mass a surface sensitive to the slightest
breath of air ; the atmosphere was electric with
the quivering heat. Never had I felt so completely
open to natural influences — never so penetrated by
the soothing yet stimulating spirit of the country.
Yet the previous night I had sat by a sickbed,
full of trouble and anxiety, and had hardly closed
my eyes. Can anyone explain why at times, when
in perfect health, easy in mind, and seemingly in
the very mood for a holiday, even amidst the
loveliest surroundings one is dull and irresponsive ;
while at others, when all the conditions seem
unfavourable, one is conscious quite unexpectedly
of the keenest pleasure ? Whatever the reason of
this, to every true worshipper of Nature she gives
sometimes these supreme moments, which can never
be predicted, and certainly never forgotten. " A
perfect summer day," says a modern writer, "does
far more to restore the wounded warrior who
has fallen out of the fight — disheartened and
troubled by the desertion of friends, the falseness
of his nearest and dearest — than any amount of
human sympathy ; and in such enjoyment the
world seems powerless to harm us."

Presently the road was thrown into cool shadow
by clumps of tall trees; and there stood a splendid
red-brick Tudor mansion with gables, turrets, and

twisted chimneys, surrounded by shaven lawns through which a little river wound, with a background of sunlit meadow. This was Faulkbourne Hall. It was here that Mr Hissey, on one of his driving tours, was so surprised and hurt at the polite refusal of his request to see the interior of the house, in the course of a chance visit ; it being not unnaturally regarded by its owner rather as a private dwelling than as a historic monument. An excellent architectural authority finds nothing in the building earlier than about 1500 although one of the historians of Essex describes the tower gateway as " a fine specimen of early Norman. " As to the church, which stands within the park, a stone's throw from the Hall, at the edge of the road, there can be no doubt whatever ; it is a little plain Norman building, probably built by Hamo Dapifer, a nephew of the Conqueror, to whom the parish belonged at the date of the Domesday survey.

The road led me at length to White Notley — a village to fall in love with at first sight. The first object that attracted me was a water-mill whose wheel — since, alas ! grown silent — was turned by a stream coming down from a pond high up in the grounds of the Hall, surrounded by the nut-trees from which the village probably took its name. Following a bend in the road I came to a little inn with the sign of the *Cross Keys* — perhaps the church hard by was dedicated to

St Peter — and roses climbing around its porch. Entering, I was quickly served with delicious bread and cheese and home-brewed ale, brought in upon a tray covered with a spotless cloth ; and on departing, well pleased with my entertainment, I was mulcted in the exact sum of fourpence-half-penny.

And so, by pleasant footpath and broad green lane, to Fairstead, the home of ancient Tusser, whose rhymes embodying in quaint phrases much homely country wisdom, are little read now, though some of them have passed into daily speech. The place deserves its beautiful Saxon name. It stands, embosomed in trees, upon a slight hill, overlooking a gently undulating country of pasture and tillage. Its church contains some very curious faded frescoes, representing probably the events of Holy Week. The fabric itself is of Norman date, of an interesting type, many examples of which are to be met with in Essex. Mr Chancellor gives the following points by which they may be recognised. The walls are invariably three feet thick. The pebbles built into the walls are laid in horizontal courses. The quoins are square — that is, there are no buttresses. Another interesting feature about these small but solid structures is the amount of Roman brick worked into them especially at the corners and at the edges of round-arched doorways. Whence was this material derived ? The spade has proved that most of

these village sites have been inhabited from very
early times — most of them being on hilly ground
and near to running water. In many of them —
as in the vicarage garden at Fairstead — remains
have been unearthed which show that a Roman
villa at one time stood on the spot. The remains
of such buildings formed in later times the quarry
from which was derived a material very useful in
a district largely devoid of stone.

A few miles to the east of Fairstead, I found
another church of this description, but with an
added charm. From the churchyard-gate to the
south door were a beautiful avenue of lime-trees,
which our fathers seem to have loved to plant in
this position; and I think there are no trees in the
world which give so delightful a shade. While I
rested in the porch at Cressing, I remembered the
cell or preceptory of the Knights Templars which
formerly existed in the parish, and afterwards
belonged to the Hospitallers of St John of Jerusalem, and bethought me of the words of old
John Stow : " Their profession was, besides their
daily service of God, to defend Christians against
Pagans, and to fight for the church, using for
their habit a black upper garment, with a white
cross on the fore part thereof ; and for their good
service were so highly esteemed, that when the
order of Templars was dissolved, their lands and
possessions were by parliament granted unto these,
who after the loss of Jerusalem recovered the Isle

Cressing — The Church of All Saints.

Cressing Temple — The Great Wheat Barn.

of Rhodes from the Turks, and there placed themselves, being called thereof for many years Knights
of the Rhodes ; but after the loss therof, 1523,
they removed to the isle of Malta, manfully opposing themselves against the Turkish invasions. " I
found the farmhouse known as Cressing Temple a
mile or more away, but could see nothing dating
from the time of these valiant knights except two
immense barns, built of massive timber, probably
of the fifteenth century, and a portion of the moat.
But at Little Maplestead, some ten miles to the
north, a village which formerly also belonged to
the Knights Hospitallers, a church built by them
still stands — the smallest of the four ancient round
churches now left in England. This circular building is divided into an inner nave and an external
aisle by six light clustered piers, supporting pointed
arches. Although much of the building has been
restored of late years, it remains of the highest
interest. Yet I think that I realised the life of
this ancient order of knights even more at Cressing.
The mighty barns reminded me that these men,
when their doughty deeds were done, lived upon
their lands, like the members of the other religious
orders, and rejoiced in the ripening of the harvest
and the garnering of the sheaves. And as I
returned towards Witham for the night, my path
lay through the standing wheat, which glowed in
the level rays of the setting sun. A great peace
seemed to have fallen upon the earth. Hardly a

sound was to be heard, not even a house was in sight. Only when alone can one fully absorb that most impressive thing in all nature — the sentiment of sunset over corn. Is this misanthropy, a severance from the life of one's fellows ? Surely not, for here is that which is to feed them. It is the blending of man's labour and man's need with the fruitfulness and glory of the universe that grips us so strongly where our spirits have room to breathe.

After I had reached my inn at Chipping Hill I wandered forth again to view the village in the fading light. At twilight I found myself on a steep grassy slope near the railway ; and looking about me, was suddenly struck by a curious curving ridge in the ground some distance below, which looked like a fragment of a perfect circle. By pure accident I had lighted upon the ancient entrenchement or camp, maybe that thrown up by the forces of Edward the Elder, or possibly by men of earlier date. Such a joyful discovery falls now but seldom to my lot, since I have contracted the habit of finding out something about the antiquities of a place before I visit it.

Next day I proceeded to Kelvedon, where a bridge spans the wide sluggish Blackwater, and where stands the quaint old inn beneath whose roof was born — strangely enough — the preacher Spurgeon. Beyond Kelvedon, at the end of a bewildering tangle of lanes, I found the famous Tower of Layer Marney. There is a peculiar pathos about this place, which stands still unfinished in all the stateliness of moulded brick and terra-cotta, very much as it was left by its builders four hundred years ago. Its turreted gateway, rising above the trees in one of the most secluded corners of Essex, tells the story of the short lived splendour of its founders, an old and knightly race who rose to greatness only in an age when other than the knightly virtues ruled, and fell for ever. The Marneys were of Norman stock, but achieved no renown until the reign of Henry the Eighth, at whose accession one Henry Marney was Sheriff of Essex and a Privy Councillor. Gaining the king's favour by his skill as a courtier, he was made Captain of the Bodyguard, Knight of the Garter, and a Baron with the title of Lord Marney. Upon the ancestral acres he began to build a house which should fitly reflect the lustre of his family, but died before the work was done. His son John, who succeeded him, died also a year later, and with him died the last of the Marneys. Now in the death-like stillness of the church which stands beside the house, under the shadow of some ancient elms, they rest in armour upon their canopied tombs, with hands uplifted in perpetual prayer.

As I left Layer Marney, and struck westward, the lanes led up to the high bare plateau of Tiptree Heath. Now largely under cultivation, thanks no doubt to the example of the scientific agriculturist Mechi, this heath was formerly a wilderness of gorse and furze inhabited chiefly by gipsies. These nomads were said to be in league with the smugglers who drove a thriving trade on the coast. Cargoes of contraband goods, run by night into the creeks that abound in the Blackwater estuary, were transferred to the backs of donkeys and ponies which would be seen in the morning quietly browsing near the smoky tents. Many a coastguardsman, it is said, who showed himself particularly inquisitive, had a bullet put into him while crossing the heath, and was seen no more on His Majesty's errands.

The gipsies and smugglers have gone now, and one may traverse the whole length of the heath without adventure. The inns which may here and there be met with are of the poorest description, a rare thing in Essex, and only explained by the former character of the district. The toilsome way is rewarded by views over the wide gleaming Blackwater from the highest points, until at length the road descends, and crosses the river where it runs, a comparitively narrow stream, through a well-wooded valley.

On the day when I pursued this road, my destination was Hatfield Peverel. The afternoon was stormy, and the thunder was still rolling at intervals, although the rain had ceased. I passed up the avenue, and entered the park, with its undulating greensward, its noble clumps of trees, and spreading lake. Over all was an indescribable freshness and peace. The house, standing on a slight rise, amongst dark cedars, appeared to be unoccupied, and I plucked a pale rose from a bush growing round the iron balustrade of the porch. Turning towards the church, which stands not far from the house and well within the park, I noted the blocked-up round-headed west doorway, and went in at the north door. In the north aisle I saw the curious stone effigy to which so strange a story is attached. Ingelrica, a celebrated Saxon beauty, and a daughter of Ingelric, became the mistress of William of Normandy. Afterwards she married Ranulph or Ralph de Peverel, one of William's retainers, by whom she had three sons. The Conqueror granted this manor to Peverel ; and here, in atonement for her sins, Ingelrica founded a college or priory, dedicating it very appropriately to Mary Magdalen. The priory stood where the house now stands : the priory church — in spite of subsequent changes — is the same. The stone effigy of a woman is said to represent the foundress, although this may be doubted. Yet the story of a ruder and simpler epoch gains wonderfully in interest as one looks around upon the contemporary structure that rose out of it ; while the details of round chancel arch and narrow splayed windows take on a new meaning, and remind us that the very stones of vanished ages are in truth alive.

XIII

The Heart of Essex

" A second crop thine acres yield,
Which I gather in a song. "— *Emerson*

WHEN you have wandered for days amidst the wheat, you begin to understand why Chelmsford which stands in the heart of it, is the county town of Essex. There is no busier place in the world than Chelmsford on a market-day. Here the broad-shouldered husbandmen, clad in tweed and homespun, whom you may have met on their lonely farmsteads or in the warm parlours of village inns, bring samples of their produce, and in a babel of homely speech determine for the rest of the world the price of its daily bread.

As though resolved to maintain its business reputation, Chelmsford has swept away most of its antiquities. Of these only a few old coaching inns are left. Its public buildings are of Georgian Ionic, and the chief interest of its streets is found in the shop windows. To go back to its earliest history, the Romans have left their traces in tesselated pavement and funeral urns, but their great road swerved aside and ran through Writtle.

118

From early Saxon times there was, no doubt, a ford over the Chelmer, just below its confluence with the Cann. At the end of the eleventh century a bridge ws built by Maurice, bishop of London, to whose see the parish then belonged, and this diverted the main stream of traffic into its present channel. The high road to Colchester and Harwich now runs through the town, and an infinity of tributary thoroughfares converge towards it. Curiously enough, there is no branch railway from Chelmsford either to left or right, so that around the county town the roads are still of importance and the country singularly unspoilt.

One summer morning I started out of Chelmsford by the northern road with a long day's tramp before me. The first halt was made at Broomfield, a little village surrounding a green, on whose gravelly soil the broom plant probably grew of old. The church has abundance of Roman brick worked into its walls, and a round tower of Norman age. From hence the road ran along the valley of the Chelmer. Presently I came upon a delightful park, with the river flowing through it, and deer and cattle browsing in the shade of the trees. This beautiful place, known as Langleys, is said to have been staked upon a throw of the dice, and lost, by Sir Richard Everard, the last of the old Essex family of Everards in 1705. It stands in the parish of Great Waltham. The single street of the village, with ancient houses and small shops,

winds around the spacious green churchyard. Here
I found a litter of planks and ladders with work-
men busy at repairing the church. What was
intended I do not know; certainly little mischief
could be done to the massive Norman tower, the
finest feature of the building, and as to the fate of
the Perpendicular and still more modern detail I must
own myself indifferent. It was now high noon.
Throwing myself down on a grasssy bank under
the shade of a spreading oak just outside the
village, the murmur of the Chelmer was in my
ears, and the old water-mill built over the river-bed
showed its irregular gables over the willows. The
hum of insects in the drowsy heat lulled me as I
lay stretched on the grass, and a rare temptation
assailed me unawares. Why should I not rest here all
day if I choose ? Why toil any more along
the hot and dusty road ? Why slavishly worship
an Itinerary of my own devising ? Then the
spirit of obstinacy asserted itself ; the hatred of
being beaten brought me to my feet again, and
set me once more upon the blinding road. Presently the road began to rise, the trees grew fewer,
and on the stony ground beyond the hedge I heard
the peculiar shuffling sound that marks the presence
of a flock of sheep. A mile or two of this, and
then a dip to the river again ; up another hill, and
Felstead came into view. The cold slate roofs of
the modern school-buildings mar the picture as
one approaches the town ; which otherwise is a

pleasant old place enough, distinguished from others like it by the curious lantern which surmounts the tower of the church. At the head of the street the road parts right and left ; and at the left corner, placed obliquely so as to command both thoroughfares, hangs the pictorial sign of the *White Swan.* In an upper chamber of this ancient hostelry I had my midday meal. Opposite the window where I sat was an old shop, at the door of which stood a figure of Atlas supporting the upper storeys, and on the carved beam above the ground floor I read the legend–GEORGE : BOOTE : MADE : ME : 1594. On the other side of the road was a long, low, tiled and plastered building in which of old the famous school was carried on. In the middle of this was a Tudor archway giving access to the churchyard and leading to the south door of the church. I found this door locked, and went in search of the clerk. He, good man, had gone for a long drive with his wife, and taken the key with him. So I had to postpone till a later visit my survey of the interior, with its interesting work in the Norman and Early English styles and in the intervening Transitional. I had also to omit seeing the elaborate tomb of the man who founded Felstead School in 1554 ; and the two engraved marble tablets which represent him, first on horseback surounded by his retainers, and secondly on his deathbed, with priests and weeping friends. This was Richard, Lord Rich, High

Chancellor to Edward the Sixth, who died in 1568 Doubtless, zeal for the New Learning had much to do with the rise of grammar schools at this period, but they were also perhaps a salve to the consciences of the men who sacked the abbeys and priories, of whom Lord Rich was notably one. Yet as Professor Thorold Rogers says : " I am convinced that schools were attached to every monastery, and that the extraordinary number of foundation schools established just after the Reformation in 1547 was but a fresh and very inadequate supply of that which had been so disastrously extinguished. " Three sons of Oliver Cromwell were educated at Felstead, and Robert Cromwell, who died in 1639, was also buried here.

Just outside the town I saw an oast-house, with its quaint contour and mellow colouring. This is a rare sight in Essex, as hops are no longer grown there, although until recently they might be found in many parts of the county, especially in the north. It is in the production of malt rather than of hops that Essex has excelled, contributing thus its quota to what has always been the national beverage of Englishmen. It may here be recalled that the Essex soil has proved itself capable of bearing not only the hop, but the vine. It is certain that the Romans cultivated it; while as regards its re-introduction by the Norman French, it appears that Aubrey de Vere had a vineyard at Hedingham and Geoffrey de Mandeville another at Great

Waltham.   And there is historical evidence that
the wine was drunk.

Not forgetting Felstead and Lord Rich, I made
my way by the fields and lanes to Leighs Priory.
The original priory of course has gone; Lord Rich
demolished it three centuries and a half ago, and
built upon its site a splendid mansion which in its
turn has come to ruin.   Beautifully situated in a
valley on the river Ter, surrounded by walled
gardens, and by fish-ponds, now dry, probably dug
by the monks, all that remains of the Tudor house
is a fine, red-brick, embattled gateway with ornamental chimneys, in a pitiful state of neglect, used
indeed as a pigeon house.   Cattle stand in the
muddy straw which strews the forecourt.   The
farm is now the property of Guy's Hospital ;   so
that its revenues are again devoted after centuries
of change, to the service of the sick and needy.

Following another field-path, I crossed the high-way,
and keeping close to the river, came presently
into the village of Little Leighs, which nestles on
either side of a bridge.   The small Early English
church with its white spire stood perched upon a
knoll at the head of the village.   Restoration had
made it rather spick-and-span, but left untouched
the unique wooden effigy in priest's garments.   At
the door of the school the mistress looked out, and
seemed glad to have a chat, while the eager eyes
of the restless children scanned the unaccustomed
figure of a stranger.   They were just going to

have a week's holiday to help in the pea-picking she told me ; a regular thing at that time of the year.

The first house I came upon in the scattered parish of Great Leighs was a tavern — rather large for a roadside inn — standing at a four-wont way, under the sign of the *Saint Anna's Castle*. This sign puzzled me until I learned that here formerly stood what was known as Saint Anne's hermitage. The house is said, on what authority I know not, to be the oldest licensed public-house in England. It was very bare and forlorn within, and my tea was roughly though very civilly served.

Two miles further south was the church of Great Leighs, standing in an unusual position, namely in the valley by the river ; and here was another round tower, like that at Broomfield. Near the bridge some men on ladders were busy at work not often seen — roofing a new house with thatch. They hesitated how to direct me to reach New Hall, which seems on the map but a little way off. Guided by instinct as much as anything, I found my way across the fields, through standing wheat, by woods and pastures, and reached it at last in the sunset. Here amidst tall trees and gardens stands the Hall, not a quarter of its original size, but still wearing much of the stately aspect of what was probably the finest of Essex Tudor houses. Built about 1500, the date of Layer Marney, it was acquired by Sir Thomas

Boleyn, father of the ill-fated Anne, who made it over to his royal son-in-law. Henry was charmed with it, made large improvements, and named it Beaulieu. Over one of the doors his arms are cut in stone with a pompous inscription in Latin which tells us that " King Henry the Eighth, renowned in arms, erected this sumptuous building. " His daughter Mary lived here before she came to the throne. In the next century the Parliament sold it for five shillings to Cromwell, who, however, used it but little, as he preferred Hampton Court. Now for the irony of events. In 1793, after the French Revolution. the sisters of the Order of the Holy Sepulchre. fleeing from Liège, took refuge here, and have remained ever since. The splendid central hall, now used as a chapel, is that in which the lascivious king in 1524 celebrated the Feast of St George.

Leaving New Hall amidst its peaceful surroundings in the fading light, I followed a path by the high park wall and over many more fields to Springfield. In the dimly lit church the points of architectural interest were hardly visible ; while on the greensward without, wholly uninterested 'in architecture, a number of clear-voiced boys were playing, waiting for choir practice to begin. And so I came to the brightly-lit shop windows and lively streets of Chelmsford.

Early next morning I sallied forth again ; and passing the ivied grey stone tower of Great

Baddow, went abroad whither fancy led me into the lovely wooded country east of the county town. At length I came to where the houses of a little hamlet lie scattered upon a slope dominated from afar by the long hill and spire of Danbury. Here in the midst of a field of oats stood a tall Transitional arch, the sole remaining fragment of what must once have been the noble priory of Bicknacre. The farmer in whose field it stood told me that the foundation of other parts of the building could be made out, and that while any portion of the original priory remained above ground, his own and four other neighbouring farms escaped payment of tithe.

A city set upon a hill cannot be hid; and it was easy to find the way to Danbury. After lunch at the *Griffin*, one of the oldest and best inns in Essex, I traced what can yet be seen of the circular encampment in which, at the summit of the hill, the church and village stand. On the north side the fosse is thirty feet deep. The view from Danbury — which stands some seven hundred feet above sea-level — is as lovely a sylvan landscape as one would wish to see ; but though I spent the whole afternoon in looking at it, I remember nothing but an infinity of trees and sunshine.

Returning by the westward road, down the long descent to the bridge which spans a little tributary of the Chelmer, past the brick tower of Sandon,

which glowed softly in the evening light, I came
out at last upon the open common at Galleywood.
Here I fell in with a boy of about twelve years,
who took my fancy greatly with his bright face
and intelligent talk.   He had lost his parents, he
told me, and was living with his grandfather, who
followed the good old trade of a wood-cutter.   He
took me to the little lonely cottage among the
trees, and persuaded his grandmother to prepare
some tea for me.   The old man brought in some
faggot-wood to make the kettle boil, and explained
to me how the greater heat given out by sticks
with the bark on them was due to the *heart* in the
wood.   He was a little reserved at first, but presently talked freely and with much shrewdness
upon men and things; showing that grasp of
essential facts which is given to men of natural
intelligence living simple and quiet lives.   So we
sat and talked far into the dusk.   When I rose to
leave, and stepped out into the shadowy woodland
road, they all came to the garden gate and bade
me good-night.   I have never seen them again,
but I often wonder what has become of that
boy.

XIV

From Dunmow to Thaxted

"Only as we gaze upon their silent figures sleeping upon their tombs, some faint conceptions float before us of what these men were when they were alive; and perhaps in the sound of church bells, that peculiar creation of mediæval age, which falls upon the ear like the echo of a vanished world."—*Froude.*

CONCERNING " Robert Fitzwater, a valiant knight, " the old chronicler Stow tells us that " there arose great discord between King John and his barons, because of Matilda, surnamed the Fair, daughter to the said Robert Fitzwater, whom the king unlawfully loved, but could not obtain her, nor her father would consent thereunto, whereupon, and for other like causes, ensued war through the whole realm. The barons were received into London, where they greatly endamaged the king ; but in the end the king did not only therefore banish the said Fitzwater, amongst other, out of the realm, but also caused his castle called Baynard, and other his houses to be spoiled ; which thing being done, a messenger being sent unto Matilda the Fair about the king's suit, whereunto she would not consent, she was poisoned ; Robert Fitzwater and other being then passed into

128

Danbury — The Griffin.

Danbury — The Church of St John the Baptist.

France. . . . It happened in the year 1214, King John being then in France with a great army, that a truce was taken betwixt the two kings of England and France for the term of five years ; and a river, or arm of the sea, being then between either host, there was a knight in the English host that cried to them of the other side willing some one of their knights to come and joust a course or twain with him :   whereupon, without stay, Robert Fitzwater being on the French part, made himself ready, ferried over, and got on horseback, without any man to help him, and showed himself ready to the face of his challenger whom at the first course he struck so hard with his great spear that horse and man fell to the ground ;   and when his spear was broken he went back to the King of France ;   which when the king had seen, ' By God's tooth, ' quoth he (after his usual oath), ' he were a king indeed that had such a knight. '   The friends of Robert, hearing these words, kneeled down, and said, ' O King, he is your knight, it is Robert Fitzwater. '   And thereupon the next day he was sent for, and restored to the king's favour, by which means peace was concluded, and he received his livings, and had license to repair his castle of Baynard, and other castles. "

This singularly naïve account of the events which led to the granting of the Great Charter shows at least the affection in which Robert Fitzwalter was held by the chronicler of London ;

a tradition of the time when Fitzwalter was cas-
tellan and chief banneret of the city. As head of
the rebellious barons he was styled Marshal of the
Army of God and of Holy Church, and he seems
indeed to have been one of the noblest knights of
his age. These things give a peculiar interest to
the traces of him which we come across in Essex.
One of his manors was at Little Dunmow. Here,
a century before his time, a priory was founded by
the lady Juga, sister of Ralph Baynard who built
the castle known as Baynard's at Blackfriars in
London. Of this priory nothing now is left, but
portions of what must have been a magnificent
priory church are incorporated in what is now the
church of the parish. Here Robert Fitzwalter
was buried, and here are alabaster effigies of his
ancestors Walter and Matilda Fitzwalter. It is
worth while to try to realise what manner of
man it was, who, according to immemorial belief,
founded here the famous custom of the Flitch of
Bacon. Bearing in mind Stow's legend about
King John and Matilda the Fair, is it stretching
fancy too far to find a strong reverence for the
sacredness of matrimony in the ordinance reward-
ing any couple who sleeping or waking had not
repented of their marriage for a year and a day?
The flitch was given jointly by the prior and
canons and the lord of the manor, and the appli-
cants were called upon to swear, kneeling upon
two sharp stones in the churchyard, a prescribed

oath in rhyme which has come down to us. In all this ceremony is exemplified, I think, that peculiar blend of mirth and piety which is characteristic of the Middle Ages. When the spirit of mediæval life died out, this custom naturally died with it. I see nothing ridiculous in the custom as it was, but much in the modern efforts to revive it. The labours of the late Harrison Ainsworth in this direction in the middle of the last century are of a piece with those by which he sought to to galvanise a dead romanticism in the field of fiction; but they failed even more inevitably, as any attempt must fail which aims at resuscitating an ancient custom without any historical setting which gave it life and meaning. The Flitch of Bacon ceremonies which attract Bank Holiday crowds to-day depend for their success mainly upon the element of farce.

If the reader journey from Little to Great Dunmow, he will find the latter rather a dull town, with nothing very striking beyond a few old inns in its straight high street leading to the railway ; but at the northern end, where stands the spacious church, the houses are more ancient, and slope down picturesquely to the Chelmer. Though there is little in the town to detain one, the road from Dunmow to Thaxted should certainly be travelled, as it is one of the most beautiful in England. Hardly a quarter of a mile of its surface is both straight and level. It winds and dips in sinuous curves for about six miles northwards, commanding a beautiful prospect over the valley to the richly wooded heights of Elsenham and Henham. Nearly the whole way the lofty spire of Thaxted is in sight, and during the last mile or two the church and town appear in different aspects at every turn of the road. But there are two digressions that it is as well to make. I have the liveliest recollection of the charming picture formed by the village of Great Easton as I entered it from this side — a white horse looking out of his stable at the head of the street, old houses and cottages grouped on the hill leading down to the wooden bridge over the river, and beyond all, the dark green background of Easton Park. A mile further on is Tiltey, an even more beautiful spot. Here the banks of the Chelmer close in, and form one of those green sheltered nooks such as the old monks loved, where a priory formerly stood. Of this nothing remains but a fragment of wall and an exquisite church. The Decorated east window is especially fine. The loveliness and peace of the surroundings intensify the marvellous beauty of the handiwork. Such perfect proportion and grace, such due subordination of the parts to the whole, such free flowing, yet harmonious tracery, filling without even stiffnesss or extravagance the spaces assigned to it — like a flower that has opened all its petals and not yet become overblown. Surely no architecture in the world approaches Gothic at its best. One feels here that the art of design in building can no farther go, that any progress beyond this can only be downward, as the event indeed has proved. One is oppressed with the divine sadness with which we behold perfection.

Thaxted (the thatched place) is a town which has contributed no striking event to our history ; there is no particular spot in it hallowed by national association ; and yet the whole aspect of the place is eloquent of the past. It seems to have been the Sheffield of the Middle Ages, before coal had taken the place of wood as fuel. The timber of the weald country around it glowed in its furnaces, wherein were tempered the most famous knives and swords ; and one of its outlying hamlets is still called Cutlers' Green. As you enter the town from the south, the first buildings you note in the broad street are great thatched barns or ware-houses standing closed and empty. As you pro-ceed past silent houses and shops, the road divides, and at the corner stands the old Moot Hall, with overhanging upper storeys raised on stout oaken pillars. Here still hang two poles with large iron hooks, formerly used for pulling the thatch from burning houses. Behind the Moot Hall a flight of steps leads to the mound on which the church is built. This Cathedral of Essex, as it has been called, is essentially the church of a wealthy mediæval trading community, aided by the munificence of the great. In this case the chief patron was that firm friend of the manufacturers, Edward the Fourth, who seems to have finished the chancel and added the north porch, on both of which his arms are carved. The whole church has an appearance of airiness and lightness, with its elegant pinnacled spire and wide-windowed aisles and clerestories. Indeed so continuous is the line of windows in the chancel that this part of the structure seems to be more of glass than of stone. But the marks of decadence appear in the depressed arches of a style that a century or two later would cease to be Gothic altogether. One pearl of great price the church of Thaxted possesses, and that is a parish clerk who has intelligence, knowledge, and enthusiasm, a man who journeys about the country to compare other churches with his own. Travellers who have suffered under the perfunctory recitals of the average local cicerone will know how to appreciate the change. I met here another interesting character, a member of the church choir, who had just had his first experience of railway travelling, and was mightily astonished by it. So completely out of the world is Thaxted. Up to now the railway has not come within seven miles of it ; and one finds that to get at the heart of ancient England one must go out of the hearing of the locomotive whistle.

On the west of the town there is a lovely walk

through the meadows along the banks of the infant Chelmer. Further on in the same direction is the splendid Tudor mansion of Horham Hall, where Elizabeth lived for a time before she came to the throne, and where as Queen she was sumptuously enertained on one of the royal progresses of which she was so fond. It still remains a " venerable and picturesque pile of gables, turrets, battle-mented parapets, ornamented chimneys, and bay windows. " On the other side of Thaxted, and separated from it, alas ! by much land given over to docks and thistles, Little Bardfield Hall nestles at the foot of a hill. Its spacious garden, near which runs a little tributary of the Pant River, is surrounded by a waved wall, the like of which I have never seen elsewhere, except on the public road just north of Chipping Hill. The opposing curves are thought to give greater solidity and power of resistance than a straight line. Quite close to the Hall, standing in the midst of the park, and approached from the road by a splendid avenue of elms, is the little church dedicated to St Katherine. The massive square tower with narrow windows is of Saxon origin, if we may trust the owner of the Hall, Mr Richard Creed, the architect, who, by the way, is restoring with reverent care the decayed south porch of Thaxted church.

XV

Pleshey

" Get thee to Plashey. "— *Shakespeare*

PLESHEY is a very good example of those numerous places which were formerly of great importance, but are now (save historically) of no importance whatever. I found it shown in very small letters on the map, lying about midway between Chelmsford and Dunmow. Finding that the ordinary way of reaching Pleshey was to follow the high road from Chelmsford as far as Great Waltham, I naturally chose a less frequented though more circuitous route along by-lanes in the direction of Chignal and Mashbury. After most extraordinary turnings and doublings, I reached at length a high open country, whence could be discerned above the trees on a hill the flagstaff on the tower of Pleshey Church. A path over the fields led ultimately into a broad green lane making straight for Pleshey — doubtless the remains of an old and important road.

The general aspect of Pleshey, with the castle-mound dominating the village which winds round

136

its base, is strikingly reminiscent of feudal times. But it has even deeper roots in the past. Its earliest known name was *Tumbelstoun*, or *the Town of the Tumuli*, showing it to have been inhabited by the ancient Britons. There are many other signs of this, of which it will be sufficient to mention the outer embankment and ditch, enclosing the entire village within its circular span in the space of about forty acres. This feature is often overlooked. Observing a section of it behind the parsonage, I followed it completely round till I came back to my starting-point. In so doing I twice crossed the road which intersects the village : at each point of intersection a gate formerly stood. The custom of the early Celtic tribes of enclosing their town within a circular bank and ditch is referred to in a well-known passage by Cæsar. When the Romans invaded the country, they could not leave so strong a place in the hands of the conquered race, and would necessarily take possession of it themselves : that they actually did so is proved by the fragments of Roman pottery and tiles which have been dug up. It is probable, but not certain that in later centuries this stronghold was occupied by the Danes. But from the time of the Conquest we find it definitely the seat of the High Constables of England, in whose keeping it remained for about four hundred years. During this period it received its Norman name of *Plecy* or Pleshey, probably from the same root as *pleasaunce;* the castle was built, and was surrounded by its own moats and entrenchments. The intermarriages of noble families and consequent changes of inheritance are difficult to follow ; but the manor was principally in the hands of the Mandevilles and De Bohuns. The last lord of Pleshey who is known to have lived at the castle was Thomas, Duke of Gloucester, regent and uncle of the ill-starred Richard II. Finding himself becoming fast deprived of all power, and his favourites put to death, the young king determined to make away with his dangerous rival. That nobleman's tragic end is thus narrated : " The duke was at Pleshey, when the king, riding from London with a few lords and retainers, suddenly appears in the castle yard. He requests his uncle's attendance at a council the next day. The duke offers his assistance, and at once sets out with the king for London. On their way through the forest he is seized by the Earl of Nottingham, the Marshal, hurried on board a vessel in the river, and conveyed to Calais. . . . Three esquires of the earl bring him to a chamber within the Prince's Inn in Calais, and deliver him to three other of the earl's esquires and six dependents ; all having sworn to secrecy that morning at the church of Notre Dame. They tell the duke he must prepare for death : he confesses to a chaplain, and gives himself up. Five of the servants suffocate him between two feather-beds, while the sixth keeps the door; the three squires kneeling and weeping and praying for his soul. " What a picture of those turbulent times!

Students of Shakespeare will doubtless remember that in the play of *Richard II.* there are several allusions to Pleshey. One of them occurs in a speech placed in the mouth of the Duchess of Gloucester after the murder of her husband, and has a pathetic interest in showing that the ruin which after this time rapidly overtook the place had already begun:

" Commend me to thy brother, Edmund York.
Bid him—ah! what ?—
With all good speed at Plashey visit me.
Alack, and what shall good old York there see
But empty lodgings, and unfurnished walls,
Unpeopled offices, untrodden stones ? "

Of the castle there is now literally left not one stone standing upon another. No masonry whatever remains, except a bridge of flat bricks built in the form of a pointed arch slightly contracted towards the base. The castle grounds, though private property, are freely open at all times, and form a kind of natural park for the inhabitants. Turning into a path by the little post-office you come upon a wide field, locally known as the Queen's Garden, and on your left you see a bold eminence clothed from base to summit with bushes and trees. Crossing the first moat by the arched bridge, you reach an irregular ring of earth-works called the Hills ; and climbing a steep path, you cross the inner moat and arrive at the central mound or mount. This is a high and level grassy space, oval in shape, measuring sixty paces long by thirty broad. Between the trees you catch glimpses of the surrounding country which once formed the Manor of Pleshey. The shorn harvest-fields lie white around, slowly traversed by waggons laden with yellow corn. From this elevated spot the whole village lies mapped out before you, with its winding street of pretty thatched and white-washed cottages. While I sit up here in the peaceful evening, and burn incense to the spirit of the place, the gold light fades in the western sky, but I am in no hurry to go. Gradually, almost imperceptibly, one or two stars appear overhead, and lights also glimmer in the diamond-paned windows below. Every sound is carried up to me distinctly in the perfect stillness ; the heavy tread of the harvest-men returning weary from the fields, the voices of women at their doors, even the frequent gurgle and splash of the fishes in the water of the moat.

As the soft-toned bell of the church strikes nine, I descend the rough path in the gathering darkness, and return to my quarters at the *White Horse.* Its faded sign is invisible now, but it is almost equally so in full daylight. The landlord, Mr George Bohannan (the similarity of whose name to that of De Bohun is certainly a curious coincidence), is a man of considerable intelligence and knowledge, and unlocks to me the treasures of his little museum, including flint and bronze implements, pottery, etc. At the back of the premises they brew their own beer, and wholesome and delicious beer it is. I am permitted to study the process of manufacture, and learn that in the village there are no drunkards and no teetotalers. Much more might be recorded concerning this old-world place ; but I trust that the reader is already tempted to say with Shakespeare, "I should to Plashy too."

XVI

Maldon and its Memories

" Is it not almost appalling to wander in such places as these, and know that the men who made history have been here too ? "— *J. E. Panton.*

MALDON stands on a bold hill between the point Where two rivers, the Chelmer and the Blackwater, unite, and the head of the wide estuary known by the name of the latter. Its most striking aspect is seen as you approach it by water, where above the white and tawny sails of its small shipping rises a steep bank covered with red-tiled houses among which here and there a tower or spire peeps forth. If you land, and climb the winding street, you see many quaint corners and old-world alleys as you pass ; but in its principal thoroughfare the town is trying to look as modern as possible. In the midst of the High Street stands the Moot Hall, sometimes called the D'Arcy Tower, with an over-hanging clock, and a portico over the footway upheld by four stone pillars; but the face it turns to the street gives no clue to its real age, and only when you examine the interior so you realise that it is a building of the early fifteenth century.

Mount the newel staircase with its hand-rail of moulded brick, and from the leaded roof, where you are in company of the five bells that chime the hours for the town, you gain a wide view of the surrounding country. The romantic wooded heights of Danbury rise away to the west, to the north is Tiptree Heath, and eastward, with low islands in its midst, the broad Blackwater spreads out towards the open sea.

It is clear that a situation like this must always have been of importance since the dawn of civilisation. The ubiquitous Romans have left their traces ; but the real history of the place begins with our Saxon forefathers. With the struggle, which lasted for centuries, between different races from over sea, for the possession of the fertile lands lying immediately behind these great in-lets, a hill lying at the head of this estuary, and dominating the confluence of two rivers penetrating many miles inland, must have been of supreme value. And in point of fact we find that one of the most famous fights between Saxon and Dane was waged on this very spot.

The national hero, Alfred, strove continually to force his restless foes back towards the east, and ran them to earth at Mersea. Upon his death, his son Edward the Elder took up the task and built the fort at Witham. " While the Burg at Witham was wrought and getimbred, " as the Chronicle quaintly says, " King Edward went with some of his forces to Maeldune in Essex, and there lived. " Seven years later he encamped here again and strongly fortified the town. The lines of his entrenchements were plainly to be seen until lately, but are almost obliterated now by the railway. In the following year, apparently in revenge for the retaking of Colchester by the Saxon forces, the Danes of East Anglia, strengthened by Vikings from beyond the sea, attacked the garrison in Maldon. In the words of the Chronicle : " They beset the borough all round, and fought there till to the borough-folk there came more force from without to help them ; and the host forsook the borough, and fared away from it ; and then fared the men after out of the borough, and eke they that had come to them for to help, and put the host to flight, and slew of them many hundred, either the ash-men (Vikings) or others. " But it was not until near the close of the same bloody century, and in the reign of Ethelred the Unready, that Maldon attained the height of its fame. In the year 991, the Chronicle tells us, came Unlaf with ninety-three ships to Staines, and laid waste all around, and thence he went to Sandwich, and thence to Gypswic (Ipswich), and harried it all, and so to Maeldun ; and there Byrthnoth the ealdorman and his force came against him and fought with him, and there they slew the ealdorman and kept the battlefield. " Now although the men of Maldon were worsted in this fight, they fought like heroes,

Thaxted – St John the Baptist, Our Lady & St Laurence.

Thaxted — The Moot Hall.

and their deeds have been handed down in that priceless relic of Anglo-Saxon literature known as the " Song of Maldon." Of this noble poem, the historian Freeman rather bitterly says :   " Were it written in any tongue but the native speech of Englishmen, it would have won its place alongside of the battle-songs of ancient Hellas. The song is plainly local and contemporary ; it comes straight from the soul of the East Saxon gleeman of the tenth century. It is something to stand on the spot and to call up the picture of the valiant Ealdorman, lighting from his horse among his faithful hearth-band, marshalling his men in the thick array of the shield-wall, refusing to pay tribute to the Vikings, and telling them that point and edge shall judge between them. Then we see the dauntless three who kept the bridge — Wulfstan, Alfhere and Maccus, comrades in the fight in which the legend of the Tiber was repeated in sober truth by East Saxon Panta. Yet among the crowds to whom the legends of distant lands are as household words, how few have ever heard the names of the inborn heroes of our own soil ? " It is impossible here to give the song as a whole, or even to point out all its beauties. What stands out from it most plainly is the noble character of Brihtnoth, and the loyal affection he inspired in his followers, which the writer of the song apparently assumes to be the normal relationship between a Saxon lord and his

K

thanes.   It would seem that the combatants were
unable to get at each other for some time, except
by the discharge of arrows, until the Panta (or
Blackwater) was at low tide ;   when Brihtnoth, in
his " overmood, " or lofty spirit, allowed his ad-
versaries to pass the ford unmolested, and gave
them room to fight in.

> " Then the Earl began
> For his overmood
> To leave of land too much
> To the loathly people ;
> Began to call them
> Over cold water ;
> The warriors listened.
> ' Now to you is yielded,
> Go straightway to us,
> Men to battle ;
> God only wots
> Who shall hold fast
> The place of slaughter.'"

After spirited descriptions of the battle, and the
deeds of individual champions, the poet tells how
Brihtnoth received his death-wound ; and how,
uttering his dying words:

> " He to heaven looked.
> ' Thank thee, Nations' Wielder,
> For all the good things
> That I in world have had ;
> Now I own, mild Maker,
> That I most have need
> That Thou to my ghost

> Good should grant,
> That my soul to Thee
> Now may make its way,
> To Thy kingdom,
> Lord of Angels,
> With peace to journey.' ”

When Brihtnoth fell, one of his followers leapt upon his lord's horse, and fled ; which desertion brings this fierce sarcasm from the writer:

> " Godric from battle went,
> And the good man forsook
> That to him oft-times
> Horses had given :
> He leapt on the horse
> That his lord had owned. ”

But the rest of the band determined to die rather than desert their master's body.   One of them — whose home seems to have been at Stourmere, near the Cambridgeshire border — declared:

> " I this promise
> That I hence will not
> Flee a footstep,
> But will further go
> to wreak in the fight
> My lord and comrade.
> Nor by Stourmere
> Any steadfast hero
> With words need twit me
> That I lordless
> Homeward should go
> And flee from the fight. ”

As these brave men fell one by one, and their resistance became even more desperate, this is how they met their fate:

> " Mind shall the harder be,
> Heart shall the keener be,
> Mood shall the more be
> As our might lessens. "

Brihtnoth, this " loved man, " as the poet calls him, was buried at Ely Abbey, which he had helped to found.   His wife Ethelflaed offered to the church a piece of tapestry on which she had worked the picture of her husband's great deeds. As Freeman (to whose paraphrase of the song I am much indebted) says, " I wish we had it now, as well as the Tapestry at Bayeux, which is so useful for our history seventy years later. "

But we have not yet done with Brihtnoth. Only a few miles to the south-east of Maldon, on a little branch of the Blackwater known as Lalling Creek, stands a lonely farm called Lalling Hall, where the foundations of an ancient chapel may still be traced.   A few months ago the property was advertised for sale, with the manorial rights belonging thereto.   Now this very manor of Lalling was given by Brithtnoth to Christ Church, Canterbury, in the year 991, the year in which the Battle of Maldon was fought, and in which its hero died.

Following the right bank of the estuary you gain from the high ground near Steeple wide

views over the marshy valley. Two islands lie
in mid-stream — Osea and Northey — each with
its single farm, and each connected on the north
with the mainland by a rough cart-track practicable only at low water. Presently the little
village of Bradwell is reached, embosomed in
trees, with a church restored, alas ! out of all
recognition. Northward, a lane leads to Bradwell Quay, a rough wharf of timber, where
some small craft may usually be found, the
sailors on board of her doing a trade in coal
or hay with farm-labourers in charge of heavy
country carts. But eastward from Bradwell
village is another road, which, leading as it does
to nowhere in particular, you are surprised to
find of good breadth and shaded by well-grown
trees. This road ends at a lonely grange known
as Easthall ; but a broad track continues in the
same direction across the fields, following which
you reach at length that corner of the coast
where the Blackwater debouches into the ocean.
You stand at the edge of the sea-wall. Opposite
rise the wooded shores of Mersea, with the
square church-tower conspicuous among the trees ;
at your feet lies the treacherous green ooze
and slime always at the mercy of the waves ;
on your right hand spreads the expanse of protected marshland, and beyond all, sparkling to
the horizon, the open sea. Around this spot
may still be traced the rectangular fosse of a

Roman camp, identified as Othona, or as the Saxons had it, Ithancester. Here was the chief fortress of the Count of the Saxon Shore, an officer appointed by the Roman governors to ward off the attacks of the Saxon pirates. It is curious that the Saxons learned the art of naval warfare from the Romans themselves, especially from Carausius, who towards the end of the third century equipped a Saxon fleet to aid him in his rebellious enterprises. A few centuries later the Saxons were called upon to defend the shores of Britain against other piratical foes. On the edge of the wesern side of this fortification, in what seems to have been the principal gateway or *Porta Praetoria*, stands an old, loosely-jointed, stone building now used as a barn. This is known as St Peter's Chapel, or St Peter's on the Wall. If all tales be true, this dilapidated old building had much to do with the founding of Anglo-Saxon Christianity in the seventh century. Let me tell the story as I find it in the quaint English of Stow : " At length Sigebert ruled in Essex ; he became a Christian, and took to him a holy man named Cedde, or Chadde, who won many, by preaching and good life, to the Christian religion. Cedde, or Chad, was by Finan consecrated Bishop of the East Saxons, and he ordered priests and deacons in all the parts of Essex, but especially at Ithancaster and Tilburie. This city of Ithancaster

(saith Ralph Cogshall) stood on the bank of the river Pante, that runneth by Maldun, in the hundred of Danesey, but now is drowned in Pante, so that nothing remaineth, but the ruin of the city in the river. Tilberie (both the west and east) standeth on the Thames side nigh over against Gravesend. " This note of Stow's is interesting as throwing light on the origin of the " Chadwell " near Tilbury ; but he is certainly wrong in saying that of Ithancaster " nothing remaineth. " Large portions of its Roman wall undoubtedly remain ; and there is high authority for believing that this ancient stone barn is the original chapel built by Chad, and appropriately dedicated to the Apostle of the Gentiles, Peter. It is impossible to stand upon this spot, noting its position, its remains of former defences, and its broad road westward, without being impressed with the conviction that in early times it must have been a centre of busy life ; and this only accentuates the present loneliness and inaccessibility of the spot ; while the thought that this single relic that has come down to us may be the actual cathedral of the first bishop of the East Saxons almost takes one's breath away.

Another example of a chapel now used as a barn may be seen when we return to Maldon. Spital Farm, which stands on the western out-skirts of the town, takes its name from St Giles' hospital for lepers, which formerly existed on this site. Adjoining the farmhouse, and reached by crossing the straw-littered yard, the remains of the hospital, now wholly put to agricultural uses, may be found. It is of stone, interspersed with Roman brick, cruciform in plan, and at the inner points of intersection are slender shafts of worked stone, crowned in one case by a rounded capital. In the south wall are three lancet windows, two of them blocked up.

Across the fields to the north stands Beeleigh Abbey. The situation is a delightful one, just below a foaming waterfall of the Chelmer, which is crossed by a flat wooden bridge, and formerly turned the wheels of the abbey mill. The Blackwater approaches within a quarter of a mile, and a canal connects the two rivers from which the hamlet of Beeleigh seems to have taken its name. When the abbot and his monks surrendered their river-side dwelling at the Dissolution, it was not pulled down — as so often happened — and a brand-new mansion built on the site ; but the conventual buildings were adapted to the needs of their new owners. Hence the abbey to-day presents the most delightful jumble of architectural styles, with Early English windows and corbels, groined roofs, buttresses, Tudor fire-places, timbered gables, and clustered chimneys. The church has entirely disappeared, but its site is thought to have been near the old walnut-trees by the river.

Before leaving Maldon one must not omit to see the church of All Saints, with its splendid east window, its elaborate arcading on the south wall, but especially its strange triangular tower, lighted by lancets, and entered from the nave by a fine Transitional arch. The verger will surely point out to you the Cammocke monument, and will perhaps bring a ladder in order that you may inspect it carefully, for it is placed high up on the wall of the north aisle. Under a costly marble canopy of heavy seventeenth-century design you see the kneeling gowned figure of a middle-aged man, on each side of whom, their faces turned towards him, kneel two women, also past their earliest youth. Underneath are panels crowded with groups of kneeling children of all ages. These figures represent Thomas Cammocke and his two wives with their respective families. The monument was erected by the eldest son, and by the second wife, who was Lady Frances Rich, sister of Lord Rich of Leighs, afterwards Earl of Warwick. No one would think to look at this presentment of uninterrupted family life, how romantic was the story of the second marriage. Morant relates how Cammocke was in the suite of the Earl of Warwick and courted his daughter, and that in travelling from Leighs to Rochford Hall he carried her off upon a horse and came to Fambridge Ferry ; when, finding themselves pursued, the boat being on the other side, they had no alternative but to swim through nearly half a mile of salt water with a strong tide running Cammocke advised her not to venture, but she said that she would live and die with him, and took the water. When they were half over, one of the earl's servants came to the water-side, and his horse neighed; upon which the horse that carried the lovers turned round, and with much difficulty was brought to keep his course. They rode to Maldon, were wedded and bedded; and the earl said, " seeing she had ventured her life for him, God bless 'em. " The road from Fambridge comes into Maldon at a point close by this church where the lovers were joined in matrimony; and it is easy to trace the way by which they rode from the river, where the ferry is still to be found. This Essex variant of the story of Lord Ullin's daughter has the merit both of historical truth and of a happy ending; and we leave the reader to judge, in the words of the old writer, "whether his courage or her love exceeded."

XVII

The Battle River

" Blessed England! where landmarks remain."— Knapp's Life of Borrow.

Of all the varied scenery of Essex there is none that makes so subtle and lasting an impression on the mind as that of the valley of the Crouch. To one who has not seen it, how is it possible to convey an idea of its beauty? The elements of it are simple enough — a broad tidal river flowing between low hills. In other parts of England, more rugged, and generally thought more romantic, the horizon is often narrowed by the very steepness and height of the hills. Here all is different. None of the eminences that overlook the Crouch are of any height to speak of ; but they slope upwards so gradually from the wide valley between them, and the general level of the land is so low that the rise of only a few feet in the road commands everywhere a beautiful prospect. Far into the distance spread the fields with their slanting hedgerows, rank beyond rank, the furthest of them suffused in a faint haze ; to right and left the eye roves up and down the valley, resting where the light strikes on the grey tower of a church amid its clump of trees, or on the white gable of some hillside farmstead.

As it often fortunately happens, it happens here, that a district of singular beauty is bound up with cherished associations of the past. On one of the low hills that overlook the river, the battle of Assandun was fought in the year 1016, and Canute founded a church in honour of his victory. We have seen in an earlier chapter that Ashdon laid claim to having been the theatre of these events : this distinction is also coveted by three parishes near the Crouch — Canewdon, Hockley and Ashingdon. That the last-named place is the rightful claimant seems to me certain.

Still it is probable that the indications of former warfare which are so conspicuous in names and sites on the banks of this river do not all owe their origin to one particular battle. The marauders from oversea, whether Saxon or Dane, found here, as has been well observed, a congenial coast-line ; their shield-hung ships, when they approached our shores, found that the flowing tide served them for many miles inland ; and as they cast eager eyes at the thriving settlements, with ripening harvests on the slopes and grazing herds in the valleys, we may be sure that their progress was keenly scanned from the rude entrenchments on the hill-tops. Later on, some of these fortified summits became the sites of more important strongholds, as at Rayleigh. Here Sweyn, who was in possession of the place at the time of the Conquest, and was allowed to retain it, had a park and vineyard, and built a castle, the remains of which may still be seen. As you approach the village it makes a pretty picture, especially from the north ; for the church, though internally a cold uninteresting building, raises aloft among the trees a bold stone tower with a turret at one angle, surmounted by a flagstaff, and groups harmoniously with the old windmill and the green castle hill. If you climb the ramparts and cross the deep ditches — in one of which the water still stands, with a patch of lilies — and scale the almost perpendicular sides of the oval-shaped central mound, you are rewarded by a magnificent panorama. The strong air that blows over it, the bright light that surrounds it, and the height from which you survey the wide pastures around, make the place seem a perfect eyrie. You understand the sense of power and domination that must have filled the hearts of men who had such places for their dwelling.

From here it is but a few miles down the marsh roads to the head of the Crouch, where ʼstands a small hamlet called by the significant name of Battlesbridge. Tradition connects this name with the battle of Ashingdon ; and it is suggested that a bridge here may have formed the means of escape for the fugitives or the point at which the victors had to give up the pursuit.

There is nothing unlikely in the notion that there was a bridge here even in the eleventh century, for the river at this point is very narrow ; indeed, this is its highest tidal limit.   An iron bridge of one arch spans it to-day, under which, when I saw it, a thin stream was making its way through an expanse of mud.   Below the bridge was a wharf at which a barge with brown sails was moored ; above it, a disused water-mill — probably three centuries old — with bare rafters bleaching in the sun and ancient machinery inhabited by rats.

Two or three miles to the east, near some ancient barrows, lies Hull Bridge.   There is no bridge now, but there is said to be a ferry. When I reached the north bank — on which side there are no houses — the boat was of course upon the further side, where a little street of ancient houses sloped down to the water's edge.   I stood on the bank, and shouted " Ferry ! " at intervals for nearly half-an-hour.   Some men who were hard at work bulding a large boat ceased knocking ; two or three women looked out of their doors, but nothing else happened.   Clearly no ferryman was to be expected that day.   Fortunately I had not an elopement on my hands, like Cammocke, and could afford to turn back and go round another way.   It happened that my way led me near Stow Maries Church, in which there is a tomb with a brass to the Cammocke family ; and presently I came to the spot where the runaway couple landed exhausted after their perilous swim across the Crouch. This was North Fambridge, a secluded village, with shady avenues down to the water. Pea-picking was in full swing in the fields, a picturesque operation enough, but carried on by a very poor class of people, and not without discomfort, as I very soon found. For on reaching the *Ferry-Boat Inn* by the river-side, I found it surrounded by a famishing multitude. The civil landlord told me that these people, who drift all through the summer from one farm to another, wherever there is work to be got, had come into this out-of-the-way place without any provision having been made for them. His wife had gone with a cart to a neighbouring village, and presently returned with some loaves of bread ; after which the tumult subsided a little, and I was furnished with a meal in comfortable quarters usually sacred to the Fambridge Yacht Club. I heard that considerable damage had been wrought here by a flood in 1897, and that a Colonel of the Royal Engineers, who had recently come down to inspect the place on behalf of the Local Government Board, inquired the name of the river, and frankly confessed that he had never heard of it. I visited the scene of the disaster. Traversing a long narrow bridge of planks built on piles, I crossed an expanse partly of mud and partly of water, and reached a strip of grassy land lying out in the river, from whence the ferry might be taken.   A picturesque sailing-barge lay grounded on the mud ;   she was laden with chalk for the repairing of the breach. Water was rushing fiercely through the stakes that had been planted to keep in the chalk, and seemed likely to wash the whole away.   Further down the river lay Bridgemarsh Island, a large piece of the mainland cut off by a branch of the river, where lean cattle in large numbers are taken to graze, fattened, and sent to market.   The river up and down presented a rippling surface that gleamed and sparkled in the sunshine.   As the tide was flowing, I secured a passage on a barge and sailed up the stream for a mile or two, landing near Barton's farm in Hockley parish.   A long gentle ascent, followed by a short and steep one, brought me to Hockley Church, which stood among trees upon a knoll with roses and snap-dragon blooming around the graves.   Was this " curious, low, massive, octagonal tower " a relic of the original church built by Canute?   One might well believe it ;   but there was Ashingdon yet to be seen.   A pretty lane led to the top of Hockley village, near the *Bull Inn* and the blacksmith's shop.   Along the high road on either hand the little wooden cottages stood with their bright patches of old-fashioned garden, the blue smoke rising against a background of leafy trees, which in the still air of a midsummer day had an almost ethereal beauty. So it continued for about a mile until the road

Hockley — The Church of St Peter & St Paul.

Hockley — The Spa.

divided, and at the corner there was a large building with a flight of steps leading up to its central
door, over which was the legend *Spa Hotel.* Why
such a house, with such a title, in this quiet rustic
spot ? A mineral spring was discovered here in
1840, a period when English spas had not gone
out of fashion. Its medicinal virtues were proclaimed far and wide, and a hotel, pump-room, and
baths erected ; but the passion for the sea-side
was rapidly growing, and the enterprise ignomini-
ously failed. The *Spa Hotel* still keeps open its
doors, but the fashionable world never enters them,
and meditative fowls brood undisturbed upon its
threshold. A little distance down the lane a large
square edifice, faintly resembling a Greek temple,
stands forlorn in the midst of tall weeds and
thistles, with its doors and windows boarded up.
It is all that is left of Hockley Spa.

A monument of greater interest if of more
obscure history is to be found but a few fields
further on. This is an eminence near the Crouch,
known as Plumbarrow Mount. Probably raised in
commemoration of some unrecorded battle and
the bones of some prehistoric warrior, it has been
converted to modern uses by the erection upon it
of a sort of wooden summer-house, up to which
I climbed. Farms, fields, woods, and spires of
churches appeared in all directions ; the river
flowed among the trees at my feet, while far
away was the gleam of a white sail slowly moving

in the estuary, and the line of the spreading sea
beyond.   I shut my eyes, and the whole scene
was blotted out ;   then I became conscious that
the air in this quiet spot was full of sound — of
the hum of insects, voices of birds, lowing of
cattle, and all the innumerable gentle noises of a
summer's day.   I heard these things, of course,
before I closed my eyes, and they contributed, no
doubt, to the total impression of the scene upon my
mind ; but not until the sense of sight was arrested
did the world of sound assume a separate reality.

Four miles' walk to the eastward brought me to
Canewdon, in the name of which some memory of
the great Canute must surely be enshrined.   Perhaps he made it his camp on the eve of his great
battle at Ashingdon.   Here in a field just south
of the church are remains of considerable entrenchments, which originally enclosed about six acres.
I knew that this was a place of great antiquity,
where Roman urns had been dug up ;   but the
sylvan beauty of its surroundings was a pleasant
surprise.   The church is unusually handsome,
well-proportioned, and elegant in detail, but no
part of it, as it stands, has any connection with
the age of Canute.

There now remained only Ashingdon to be
seen.   As I approached it from the south, the
road rose steeply towards a large farm backed by
tall elms amidst which the church was hidden.
This was the hill up which in former times crowds

of pilgrims crawled upon their knees to visit the miraculous image that stood in the church. " The powers of the saint, " says Mr Barrett, " were specially exercised in favour of barren women; and ages after the image had disappeared, it was considered lucky to get married at Ashingdon church. " The public road led both to the vicarage and to the church, and garden roses were growing in the hedge. The aspect of the church was very striking, partly by reason of its smallness, which in village churches is often in itself a mark of age, but also from the large loose-jointed stones of the tower. This tower had bold diagonal buttresses and Early English windows with their mullions broken away. Within the church the tower was entered by a very low, round-headed door. The whole building had been much pulled about. At the line of the chancel arch the remains of clustered pillars were sunk in the wall; opposite was an old-fashioned high pulpit with guttered candles. Going outside again, I found that the whole churchyard was encircled with a ring of elms beyond which was a deep ditch full of nettles. On the north side was a stile, with a path leading down a grassy hill. A great expanse of pasture spread out to the Crouch and beyond it. To the right, the tower of Canewdon church, resplendent in the westering sun, seemed no more than a stone's throw away

Of the reputed sites of famous events, some are

unconvincing ; while at others one has the irresistible feeling : This is the spot. " As to the site of Assandun, " says Freeman, " I will not enter into any discussion. I think no one will doubt about it who has been there. There is the hill on which Edmund Ironside marshalled his army for the last battle, the hill down whose slope he rushed with his sword, as the faint echo of the ballad tells us, like the lightning-flash, leaving in this charge the royal post between the Standard and the West-Saxon Dragon, and fighting hand to hand in the foremost rank of his warriors. The Raven of Denmark had already fluttered its wings for victory ; but it was only through Eadric's treason that Edmund, in the sixth battle of that great year, found himself for the first time defeated. The spot which saw Canute's victory saw also a few years later his offering in his new character of an English king. Then arose the joint work of Canute and Thurkill, the minster of stone and lime, whose material needed to be noted in the timber land of Essex. Of that minster the first priest was Stigand, the man who won his first lowly promotion at the hands of the Dane, and who lived to be hurled from the metropolitan throne at the bidding of the Norman. " It requires no effort of the imagination to believe that this curious old church of Ashingdon is, at all events in its main fabric, identical with the minster of Canute.

XVIII

Between the Tidal Streams

" By night and day their marshy verge
The creeks uncover and submerge,
And draw into their arms the streams
That thread the country of our dreams. "

A CROWDED excursion train ; a two hours' journey with the sky growing more and more gloomy ; and a persistent drizzle on alighting — such was the prelude to what lives in my memory as one of the happiest days I ever spent. When the station at Burnham-on-Crouch was reached, I watched the dispirited passengers flock into the taverns, there perhaps to remain for the rest of the day, and chose the only possible alternative — a steady walk of twenty miles or so. As I passed through the oddly-named little hamlet of Ostend, an old man sitting by a blazing wood fire gave me a cheery greeting through his open cottage door. Beyond, the clean gravel road led by infinite turns and windings through a green quiet country, where on either hand nothing was to be seen but fields and woods, to which the vapours that shrouded the distance gave an air of mystery. Rain continued to fall through the whole of the day, the country was saturated with moisture, and the sun never for an instant showed his face ; yet the charm and freshness of that walk were indescribable. What I most remember are the wild roses, which filled the air with their sweetness, and adorned the hedges, heavy with glistening raindrops, as I wandered along the lanes. The blossoming sprays that I gathered soon faded, but the remembrance of their beauty tempts me forth into the country every succeeding June to seek for the like of them.

When I next explored this district it was in company with my boy, then a child of five. Any lively child in the course of a day exerts an amount of muscular energy compared with which a walk of ten miles is as nothing. Like his elders, he naturally tires very soon of a mechanical trudge along a dull and dusty high road ; but he will go long distances without distress if a way be chosen which leads along grassy paths and luxuriant lanes, where there are plenty of pleasant nooks to rest in from time to time, and where there is abundance of interest in the sights and sounds of country life. Stevenson elected to travel with a donkey ; but though the world has reason to be grateful that he made the experiment, he was careful not to repeat it. The American naturalist, John Burroughs, in one of his charming essays, observes that an ideal companion for a country ramble is a dog; who, he

says, takes unbounded delight in the mere act of
running about in the open air, and scents a new
adventure at every turn of the road.   The same
thing is true of children ;   but beyond this, theirs
is a human companionship, and the wisdom is not
all on one side.   For a long time after this holiday
which we spent together, my boy spoke of the
London suburb in which we lived, with its terraces
and shops, as " this world, " and of the country as
" the other world. "   It is not a truth of religion
only that to enter into right relations with the
universe one must have the spirit of a little child.

As I write of this country between the Crouch
and the Blackwater, several never-to-be-forgotten
pictures rise before me.   One is the first glimpse
of Purleigh, a glimpse such as one feels would be
a rich reward for the weariest day's tramping.
There is a stretch of common, bordered by a few
cottages on the left, while on the right rises the
smoke from a dusky encampment of gipsies, whose
lean horses stray in search of pasture.   Beyond
rises a steep green hill, divided by transverse hedges
into two or three fields, through which runs the
irregular line of a footpath leading to the summit,
where the church and little village stand boldly
out against a blue horizon.   Reaching the top of
the hill, we find that it falls sharply away on all
sides, and affords standing-room to but a very few
houses, besides the church, and a quaint cosy-
cornered inn.   A little below the summit is a

nearly perfect circular earth-work, thick with trees, and inhabited only by innumerable rabbits. In the deep ditch which surrounds it, we find the white ashes, still warm, of a gipsy fire, with a long cooking spit *in situ*, thrust slant-wise into the earth and resting upon a large stone.

Later in the same day, we are a little further to the south in a beautiful district near Stow Maries. All around us are woods, which acquire a weird and strange beauty — the trees seeming to shed light instead of receiving it — as the sky grows black with thunder. As the storm bursts we are glad to take shelter in a neighbouring cottage. Tea is in progress ; we are invited to share it, and hospitably made at home. So we sit by the open door, inhaling the fresh breath of the revived vegetation, while the lightning flashes across the wooded landscape, and the thunder rolls gradually away.

At another time we are on the sea-wall on the north bank of the Crouch. Sheltered in a fold of the hill the stately outline and mellow colouring of an Elizabethan farmhouse appear ; before us, huddled on the water-side, the old houses of a little town, yachts and boats in the river, and a coasting vessel with mast aslant moored to the bank in the foreground. This is Burnham. Beyond it lie the Hall and church, separated from the little township by nearly a mile of wild common. Further on is an ancient windmill, whose crazy timbers we tread with trepidation ; its creaking sails, alas ! are since silent. Then comes South-minster, with a church, once its pride, but now retaining little of its former greatness beyond its ample proportions. Down the long narrow street comes the town crier, ringing his bell to announce a parish meeting, and is scoffed at for his pains by young men and maidens sophisticated by the advent of the railway. Out of the town again, we see women in sun-bonnets gleaning in the upland corn-fields lately reaped. The goodness of the harvest is attested by sixteen stacks together in a row. Following a lane leading nowhere save to the marshes and the sea, we pass the little church of Dengie with its beautiful Decorated east window and exquisitely peaceful sylvan surroundings. There is continuous faint thunder over the distant ocean, and even in the strong sunshine the light-ning can be seen far off flashing like a brandished sword.

Turning to the south, we find ourselves among the seemingly interminable marshes that lie between Burnham and the sea. The great farms or " halls " stand solitary amid the broad pastures. The pastures are divided, not by hedges, but by dykes, where tall reeds and bulrushes flourish, and one can see far across the spreading levels. In one of the fields men are burning dock-leaves : a long stream of smoke ascends obliquely into the air. Going by ferry across from the mainland to Foulness Island, and afterwards from Foulness to Wallasea, we see nothing all the rest of the day but the same Dutch landscape of marshes, dykes, windmills, and cattle. Evening is upon us before we reach the last ferry, that which carries us over the Crouch to Creeksea. I sit in the stern of the rude boat, my boy between my knees, the ferryman plying his oars, and all of us silent. The river runs due east and west. On our left hand, towards the country, both river and sky are suffused with all the conceivable warm colours of a departed sunset ; while on our right, towards the sea, the watery horizon is wrapped in the cold blues and greys of advancing night. The black hull and rigging of an anchored vessel loom out of the dusk, our boat's keel slides into the ooze of the beach ; so now, still under the spell of the beauty that has just been revealed to us, we hasten along between the high dark hedgerows to seek

" A sleep

Full of sweet dreams, and health, and quiet breathing. "

XIX

South Essex: Chiefly Churches

" From Langdon's shoulder the glad beholder
Gains sweeps yet bolder o'er hill and lea,
Where, widening ever in long endeavour,
The glistening river o'ertakes the Sea. "

ON the Eastern outskirs of London, half surrounded by the wide bend of the Thames known
as Woolwich Reach, is a level tract of land of
melancholy aspect. Not that such low-lying
districts are necessarily unbeautiful : against a
bare horizon the eye rests with peculiar pleasure
upon the simplest object having harmonious lines
— a clump of trees, a cottage, or a windmill ; on
the other hand, while ugliness is softened by hilly
and sylvan sourroundings, it is painfully accentuated
by the severe contour of the flats. Here the view is
bounded by the monotonous roofs of terrace-
houses where dwell the wives and families of them
that go down to the sea in ships. But in the
midst of this desolate scene there remains an exquisite relic of other days — the little church of
East Ham. Standing quite by itself, a little back
from the road, in the midst of an ancient churchyard,
it is approached by an avenue of lime-trees just

like those we have seen at Cressing and Great Clacton, churches of contemporary age, but now so infinitely different in environment. Its broad massive tower with Norman windows, its apsidal east end with flat buttresses, tell us before we enter it to what epoch the building belongs. Passing from the tower into the nave through a tall round arch, we are struck at once by the three faint small deeply-splayed windows, which admit but a faint light into the apse. Nearly the whole of the apse is occupied by a heavy seventeenth-century tomb, and another of similar design has caused the defacement of some most beautiful arcading of intersecting arches on the walls of the chancel. The whole structure is worth going far to see ; and standing where it does, the marvel is that it has not been swept away long ago.

Hard by is Vicarage Lane, still an old-world thoroughfare, leading to a path over the marshes. Wooden bridges here and there span dykes in which the reeds forlornly rustle, and presently we come to a river, with a windmill on the left hand and the roofs of an old town in front. Near the bridge are busy flour-mills and towering wood-stacks with red-sailed barges moored near the wharf. The town is Barking, the river the Roding, here called Barking Creek. It was here that the Conqueror first took up his residence in England, after the battle of Hastings. Four centuries earlier, Erkenwald, bishop of London, founded the famous nunnery which numbered even royal women among its abbesses. Of the later buildings of the Abbey, nothing now remains but the fourteenth century gateway known as Firebell Gate, in which the curfew bell was rung, according to an ancient tradition till lately kept alive by the ringing of a bell at eight in the evening during half of the year. The gate leads into the churchyard. Deplorably modernised as a whole, the spacious church has still its handsome Decorated tower, and bits of Norman work in its chancel. As we return through the gateway and thread the narrow streets, passing the timber and plaster market-house with overhanging upper storey, we come, on the north of the town, to higher ground. Here stands Uphall, a brick farmhouse with great barns, enclosed within a rectangular entrenchment, with a rampart and mound on the west side, overlooking the river, which flows through the marshes immediately beneath, and ceases at this point to be tidal. Retracing our steps through the town, and striking into the open country to the eastward, we pass in a mile or so the famous Eastbury House, where it is said that Gunpwder Plot was hatched. Be this as it may, the house is picturesque enough with its gabled roofs, clustered chimneys, and tall octagonal tower, amidst the level pastures.

Still further to the east lies a tract of country which I had long avoided. Seen from the deck of a steamboat as one passes up or down the river, the coast of Essex looks dull and uninteresting, save perhaps at Purfleet, which is pretty enough with its white chalk cliffs and houses half hidden in trees. But when I learned that the churches in this part of the south Essex were architecturally most interesting, I went to see them ; and lo ! I was charmed with the country. I began with Rainham, a little place which boasts a church dating from the twelfth century. Forming one of the congregation one Sunday morning, I had time to admire the heavy and massive masonry, each of its square pillars, which support plain round arches, being nearly as thick as the space between them is wide. From thence I journeyed through Aveley, South Ockendon, Stifford, and Orsett, at each of which places there are remains of beautiful Norman work, especially richly sculptured doorways. Just before reaching Orsett (the horse-heath) the road takes a sudden turn, dips into a wooded valley, and crosses a clear stream running through deep grassy meadows. How strange it seemed that this was the country I had feared and shunned !

A little to the south of Orsett, and close to Chadwell, one of the missionary stations of the Saxon bishop Chad, is the celebrated Hangman's Wood. It is beautifully situated on rising ground overlooking the river and the level marshes over which in pre-historic epochs the river doubtless flowed. Here are the mysterious dene-holes, the like of which are nowhere to be found in England, save on the opposite Kentish shore. The wood is literally honeycombed with them, their deep shafts piercing vertically into the chalk, with chambers radiating from the bottom of each shaft. They are occasionally explored with the aid of pulleys and lanterns by learned archæologists, who are wholly at variance as to their origin and use. Were they merely chalk-pits, secret store-houses for grain, or hiding-places in troublous times ? In favour of the last-mentioned view, an ingenious paper was lately published by Mr A. R. Goddard. " We know, " says this writer, " that even in the Roman era the tribes were engaged in constant inter-tribal strife before they had experience of invasions on a large scale from over sea. Let us suppose that some raiding-party lighted upon the mouth of one of these dene-holes and was suspicious of its contents. What would probably happen ? They might send down a man or two to reconnoitre. If the pit were occupied, the scouts would come to trouble. If it were unoccupied, they might prowl round the entire cavity and report it empty, without any idea that it formed one of a huge confederation. If on the other hand the raiders were nervous of exploring, they might try the effect of fire, or block up the shaft mouth, and then go on their way, com-placently imagining that they had disposed of their subterranean prey. If the pit were occupied, the victims of this grim practical joke, as they smelt the smoke or saw their exit corked up, would be aware that at the end of one of the lobes of their lair there was only a thin division of chalk between them and safety, and that a few strokes of a pick would clear them a passage into another pit, with an independent exit shaft. There is no doubt that such a system of lairs might furnish a very formidable gathering place for ambushment. Blows in one pit are easily heard in others, and by this means a signal might be given below for the men ranged in each chamber to pour out unitedly, and pounce on the unsuspecting foe. With their bare feet the men of those times were probably as expert in swarming up and down the shafts by means of their foot-holes as sailors in their rigging. The foot-holes still remain in all the shafts, by means of which they passed up and down, with the assistance of guiding ropes, of which the ruts still remain in pits long since blocked up. " In illustration of his theory, Mr Goddard quotes from a well-known modern book, Victor Hugo's " Ninety-three, " an account of the use made of very similar ancient excavations in Brittany by the peasant armies during the war in La Vendée. Hugo tells us, " In that war my father fought, and I can speak advisedly thereof. . . . It is difficult to picture to oneself what these Breton forests really were. They were towns. Nothing could

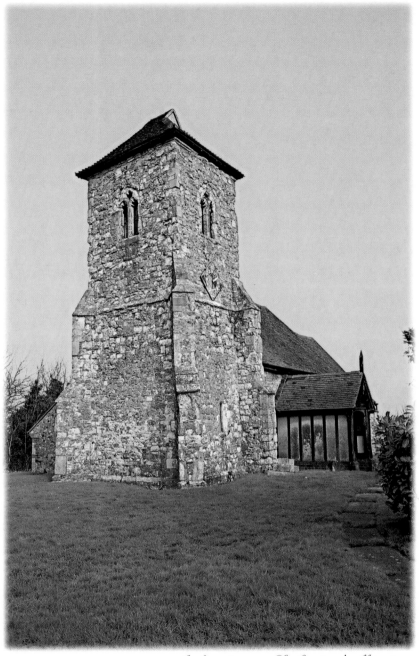

Ashingdon — St Andrew's Minster.

Mountnessing — The Church of St Giles.

be more secret, more silent, and more savage. There were wells, round and narrow, masked by coverings of stones and branches : the interior at first vertical, then horizontal, spreading out under- ground like funnels, and ending in dark chambers. . . . Each of these blind cells could shelter five or six men. . . . In Isle-et-Vilaine, in the forest of Pertre, not a human trace was to be found ; yet there were collected six thousand men under Focard. In the forest of Meulac, in Morbihan, not a soul was to be seen, yet it held eight thousand men. " The likeness between these Breton hiding-places and our own dene-holes is certainly striking. But there was nothing terrible about these cold mysterious caverns when I passed through Hangman's Wood on a day of early summer, when the blue sky smiled through the boughs overhead and the wild hyacinths through the tufted grass below.

Within a few miles northward of Orsett the character of the country varies most strangely. From the horse-heath we pass to the bull-fen — Bulphan — a wide expanse of pasture bounded by low hills and intersected by water-courses, which are crossed by brick bridges here and there : where the roads enter and leave the fen are gates to keep in the cattle. To reach the *Harrow Inn* I had to cross a bridge over a dyke full of vivid green vegetation. Hardly, however, are you out of the village, than the road begins to rise sharply up a steep stony hill.　The traveller who makes this ascent without knowing what is in store for him is to be envied.　From the top of Laindon or Langdon Hill he will see, if it be clear weather, a prospect which in its way is quite unrivalled in England.　It was of this view that Arthur Young gave so glowing a description a century ago ;　while in our own day Mr Hissey writes of it as " a glorious expanse of waving woods, green meadows, and red tilled fields ;　miles of smiling verdure, dotted here and there with scattered farmsteads, red-roofed cottages, with ever and again a peep of a distant church tower or spire. All this goodly prospect, bounded only by the circling blue of the far-away horizon. "　Save for the uninterrupted view in all directions, this prospect is quite unlike that at Danbury, with which it is sometimes compared.　The view here is over more level country, and, above all, it embraces the whole length of the Thames estuary, from London on one hand to the sea on the other.

Due north from the top of the hill, and approached by a wide green lane, is the old church dedicated to St Nicholas.　Its shingled spire rises among a clump of trees upon a little solitary knoll. Against the western end is a building of three storeys — once the dwelling of a chantry priest, and until recent years the home of a schoolmaster, who taught the children in the lowest room (which has diamond-paned windows, and is now used as a vestry,) and had his sleeping-chamber above. From the staircase by which he climbed to his attic, he had a near view of the bells and of the massive timbers of the tower, with a distant prospect of the carved oak roof of the chancel. Looking from the churchyard, the spires of Great and Little Burstead are conspicuous upon the opposite slopes, and in the valley between meanders the infant Crouch. Following the lane towards this river, we come at a cross-road to an inn bearing the curious name of the *Fortune of War*. Although the house has in recent years been rebuilt, it is an old place, and its name probably originated with the celebrated Sir John Hawkwood, who held land near here. The son of a tanner at Sible Hedingham, and apprenticed to a tailor in London, he enlisted in the army of Edward the Third, and was knighted for his valour at Poictiers. Later, as a military adventurer in Italy, he rendered signal service to the Pope, married a niece of the Duke of Milan, and died at Florence, full of riches and honours, in his seventieth year. It is believed that his body was brought home to Sible Heding- ham, and in the church there the canopy of his tomb is still shown. When last I visited the *Fortune of War*, festivities were going on in a field hard by, and I was told that this was Fortune Fair, a yearly event since time immemorial. Like many of these old pleasure fairs, it has shrunk to very small dimensions, and like many more, it will doubtless soon disappear altogether. Only the slowness with which country people change their ideas and habits can explain the survival in our days of even a vestige of the simple modes of amusement which sufficed for their forefathers. In the lonely hills near Laindon the people are still very primitive. I remember once asking for a cup of water at a little cottage after dark. The kindly old mother, and a daughter with a child in her arms, seemed to think it strange that any one should choose to roam about the hills at night, and looked at me with open-eyed wonder, almost as at a being from another world.

Eastward, the land slopes downwards to Pitsea which lies at the head of a creek, with a massive church tower standing boldly upon a bluff over-looking the innumerable channels that wind among the marshes. A little further, the church of Thundersley is reached, so small and unpreten-tious that it can hardly be seen among the trees. Yet on passing through its carved timber porch, and entering the body of the church, one is struck with the beautifully-proportioned Early English piers and arches, and especially with the sculptured capitals, representing flowers and foliage. The sculpture is wonderfully spirited, and though the general effect is harmonious, each capital is of distinct design. It illustrates perfectly that work-ing together of different skilled craftsmen for a common end, which seems to have been the secret of mediæval art. From a stile in the south-west corner of the churchyard a wide view over the marshes opens out, and a path runs down the steep hill. Following this, we arrive very soon at South Benfleet, where another church demands attention. The exquisitely-carved wooden porch is one of the most wonderful things I know ; probably nothing finer of its kind is to be found outside Nuremberg. It seems to me to breathe the very spirit of the Middle Ages.

Here at Benfleet the Danes landed in their first invasion of our shores in 874. Close by is Canvey Island, probably the *Connos* of Ptolemy. If the tide be low, you may reach it by means of planks and stepping-stones ; otherwise you must hail the ferry-man. After traversing its rough roads for a mile or two, you reach some quaint cottages of Dutch type, recalling the fact that it was a Dutchman, Joas Croppenburgh, who in 1622 reclaimed the island from the waters, receiving one-third of its six thousand acres for his pains. Already, according to old John Norden, it had been famous for its ewes' milk cheeses. With the Dutch cottages, and the Dutch dykes which divide the properties, says a modern writer, " Dutch customs survive. Teniers' favourite fiddler playing at an inn, and the people merrymaking, is often reproduced at the *Sluice House* on a holiday or harvesthome. " In his novel, " Andromeda, " the late Robert Buchanan wrote : " Flat as a map, so intermingled with creeks and runlets that it is difficult to say where water ends and land begins, Canvey Island lies, a shapeless octopus, right under the high ground of Benfleet and Hadleigh, and stretches out muddy and slimy feelers to touch and dabble in the deep water of the flowing Thames. Away across the marshes rise the ancient ruins of Hadleigh castle, further eastward the high spire and square tower of Leigh church."

Making our way back to the mainland, we reach the village of Hadleigh. This spot, once so quiet and remote that the belief in witchcraft lingered until quite lately, is now the busy scene of the Salvation Army farm colony. You pass through their territory to reach the ruins of the castle. Built by Hubert de Burgh, and destroyed in an age of destruction, probably by Lord Rich of Leighs, little of it now remains beyond fragments of two towers. These stand picturesquely enough on a steep bank, overhanging the marshy shore of the river, and having a splendid outlook over Canvey and down the broad estuary to the Nore. But the great charm of Hadleigh is its church. It has a Norman apsidal chancel with the characteristic flat buttresses ; within, a round chancel arch and curious hagioscope. With its apse dimly lighted by three splayed lancets, the church has an air of solemn mystery such as is rarely seen now in any church, and is almost always lacking in the more ambitious churches of later date. An example of the contrasting type may be seen near by at Rayleigh, where the large and well-proportioned church leaves one absolutely cold. Another is to be found a few miles further east, at Prittlewell. At the latter place is the site of an ancient priory, which gives its name to a modern mansion ; and at a cross road, amid a cluster of houses, several of them ancient, and one of them decorated with beautiful parget-work, the pinnacled tower of the church appears. When I visited it, the boy who had the key told me there had not been many " customers " that day. In the south aisle I noticed a memorial tablet to some departed worthy " of South End in this parish. " So the lively watering-place was not so long ago but a little group of fishermen's houses, an outlying hamlet of Prittlewell. In a map in my possession, dated 1610, the year of publication of Camden's " Britannia, " Southend is not marked at all. This illustrates how with all our national maritime instinct, our passion for the sea-side is essentially of modern growth. On the eastern outskirts of Southend is Southchurch, with a richly decorated Norman doorway. From here a lane leads down to the shore ; and a path along the cliffs past the coastguard station brings one to another little Norman building, the church of South Shoebury, which formerly belonged to the Cluniac priory at Prittlewell. The new streets that have sprung up

round the school of gunnery have encroached upon
the loneliness of the place. The boom of heavy
ordnance reverberates far out to sea ; steamers
trailing long clouds of smoke pass continually up
and down ; and opposite are the wooded shores
of Sheppey.

Three miles due north of Prittlewell is the old
decayed town of Rochford, at the head of the
Roach or Broomhill river. Along the road leading
westward out of the town is a magnificent avenue,
nearly a mile long, chiefly of oaks and elms, planted
by Sir James Tilney ; and the citizens have done
their part by placing seats at intervals in the shade
of the trees. At the head of the avenue the church
and Hall stand close together. The body of the
church is of stone, the tower of brick. I last
visited it on a showery Sunday morning; and while
the parishioners raised their voices within, in the
park hard by men were playing golf under the
shelter of umbrellas, while a mixed crowd of
caddies and lookers-on hung round the door of
the Hall. For the stately turreted old place
begins to look dilapidated, having fallen on evil
days ; and a farm-bailiff now occupies the home of
the Rich and Boleyn families, where it is even said
that the ill-fated Anne was born. It would be interesting to know who originated the celebrated
Whispering Court, which was held on this manor
for centuries, and until quite recent years. It was
held in the open air on King's Hill, near the town,

between midnight and cock-crow, on the first Wednesday after old Michaelmas Day. The steward opened the court in a low voice, all business was transacted in whispers, the minutes were written in charcoal instead of ink, and absentees heavily fined. Was it the outcome of a spirit of freak, as many mediæval customs seem to have been, or of some conspiracy against the lord, which he detected and punished, and the memory of which he thus perpetuated as a warning?

Eastward from Rochford, a long, winding, and ascending road leads to the little village of Barling. The church tower and spire are of graceful proportions, and crown the hill most beautifully, overlooking on the other side the marsh islands and the shining creeks with their brown-sailed craft. The general aspect of the church reminded me greatly of that at Layer-de-la-Haye, near Colchester, which is so admirably situated and conceived that it seems almost a part of nature, rooted in the earth, and tapering up into the sky.

Still further east is Great Wakering. A mile of lonely road beyond the village ends abruptly on the sea-wall at a point known as Wakering Stairs, overlooking the dreary expanse of the Maplin Sand. This seems to be the end of the world ; but is it ? Not quite. At low tide you may cross the sands to Foulness Island. One of the most curious sights I have ever beheld was when reaching the Stairs just before dusk, there appeared a procession of market-carts rapidly driven across the sands, amid much splashing, through water about a foot deep, with two or three fishing-smacks beyond and a distant steamer on the horizon. Having been on Foulness Island before, I did not attempt the journey. Walter White successfully accomplished it, but in broad daylight. Quite recently the rector of Foulness, although he had often crossed the sands before, had a very narrow escape from drowning, which he described in a letter to a friend, since published. It was all in the day's work, as he was returning from a ruridecanal conference at Leigh. " Leaving Shoeburyness at about 5.30 p.m., " says Mr Marsh, " I walked in a drenching rain to Wakering Stairs, reaching that spot about 6.30, almost completely wet through. Here I took off my boots for a four-mile walk across the sands, all under water. It was raining hard, and the sands were nearly dark, but I thought if I could reach the first broom, I could find my way across. Brooms are placed about every thirty yards, and there are three hundred and sixty-six of them. I floundered through the deep mud more than ankle deep till I reached safely the first broom. I was wet through with fresh water downwards, pouring down from hat and coat-sleeves, and salt water upwards, my boots slung over my neck, and in my hands two heavy bags of books. . . . However, I trotted along very happily for a couple of miles. I had crossed one creek and reached the second when suddenly the rain changed to a sort of Scotch mist and I could not see the next broom. But I trudged on in a straight line for ninety steps, when I found another broom. Two must have been washed away. I was very pleased, and went gaily on again, but it got hopelessly dark, and after going about forty steps and not finding the next broom, I turned back, as I thought, to find the next broom, but I missed it. The mist was then quite bewildering, and I thought I would make straight for land whatever happened. On I went for ever so far, quite lost, when suddenly to my joy I came upon a broom. Just then a black darkness came over, and I could see nothing, but I stuck to my broom, if only I could find the next. . . . I knew the tide was rising, and unless it cleared a bit, my only hope was in feeling carefully which way the waves came, and so perhaps finding the shore. " after describing how he was completely puzzled by the unexpected positions of the Swin, Mouse, and Nore lights, Mr Marsh continues : " Soon, to my delight, I reached the black mud. I pushed through it, over my ankles in slime, and every now and then stepping into a small rill. At last I reached the Saltings. They looked blacker even than the mud, and I was not certain of them at first, but sure enough I put my foot on firm vegetation. I was truly thankful. " Surely nothing could give a more vivid impression than this of the wildness of this part of the coast. But, as the reader already knows, there is another road to Foulness. Inviting the same friend to visit him, the rector writes : " Are you a good walker ? From Burnham you walk four miles along the sea-wall, and then look out for a small oyster watch-boat. You shout to the man, and he will put you over for fourpence, unless it is too rough. I have had to sleep on the boat owing to the wind, and my servant once had to do the same owing to fog, but as a rule you can cross. About two miles over fields and ditches will bring you here after landing. I can only promise a warm welcome to atone for a rough journey."

XX

The Forest of Essex

" A forest fit for dreamland. "— *J. E. Panton.*

In old Arthurian romance the adventurous knights are continually represented as riding all day through the forest, and coming now and then to a " fair town. " Perhaps this picture is not altogether a fanciful one. Early England must very largely have consisted, as newly-discovered countries are still found to consist, of forest and swamp. Perhaps we shall not be far wrong if we think of the settlements in Essex, down to the Saxon period and beyond, as oases of homesteads in small cultivated areas surrounded by large tracts of unreclaimed waste. At all events it is pretty certain that some time after the Conquest the Forest of Essex, as it was called, covered nearly `the whole of the county. By a charter of King John, confirmed by Edward the Fourth, all that part of the forest which lay to the north of the great highway from Bishop Stortford to Colchester was disafforested. Its limits were further reduced by a preambulation made in the year 1640. I have no doubt that many of the parks now existing in the county were originally merely enclosed portions of the forest; for the mediæval lords, as monarchs in their own domain, loved room in which to follow the chase. But as this process of shrinkage went on, that part of the forest lying in the south-west corner of Essex was the last to be touched. For one thing, it is the real kernel of the forest. It consists of a long strip of high broken ground, a natural fastness, hemmed in between the Lea and the Roding, which rivers flow within a few miles of each other as they approach the Thames. Moreover the successive sovereigns more jealously preserved their rights over this part of the territory than over the rest, because it lay so near to London and afforded them the pleasures of hunting within easy distance of the Court. As the forest of Essex became restricted to these narrower limits it began to be known as Waltham Forest. Waltham (the forest-town), with its splendid abbey, was the place of greatest importance within its limits, and over many of the forest manors the Waltham monks held sway. When the monastery was dissolved, the town dwindled in consequence, and at the same time the forest receded from it ; then the forest became identfied with another town more immediately within it, and acquired its present name of Epping Forest. Now Epping itself is hardly within the boundaries. It is a pleasant old market-town, standing on a high plateau, with a

wide common just to the south of it, and overlooking the stretch of woodland which bears its
name.

Many roads run across the forest in the direction
of Waltham. As you emerge from the trees upon
its western edge, and look over the cultivated
country that slopes towards the Lea, you may
see the red roofs of the old town veiled in a
haze of smoke. The presence of the government gunpowder factories has spoilt the landscape and given an air of sordidness to the
town. However, on the side next to the forest,
the country is still surprisingly fresh and untouched. The town itself has still rather an
old-world aspect with a few pleasant houses and
one or two ancient inns grouped round the
market-place. The low squat tower of the
church gives no hint of what is to be found
within. Here, it is true, what one finds is but
a relic of the magnificent building that once
was ; but what a relic ! Perhaps the effect of
the great semi-circular arches, and of the massive round piers boldly scored with spiral and
zig-zag lines, is heightened, if anything, by
the juxtaposition of tawdry modern ecclesiastical
furniture. There is no longer to be seen the
black marble slab, inscribed with the words
HAROLD INFELIX, which marked, so tradition said,
the grave of the last of our Anglo-Saxon kings.
We know that he was a generous benefactor to

Waltham Abbey, and that he offered up his vows here before the fatal battle of Hastings. Of the few remaining fragments of the abbey buildings outside the church, that known as Harold's bridge is doubtless of a later age than his. A fine gateway yet stands, and the abbey mills on the river are still grinding corn.

East of the Roding, another portion of the forest formerly existed, known as Hainault, or the high wood. It was a wild and beautiful district until the middle of the nineteenth century, when it was disafforested by Act of Parliament. The deer were driven out of it, a hundred thousand trees were felled, more than ten thousand acres ploughed up, and roads of mathematical straightness were cut through it. In Hainault Forest stood the celebrated Fairlop Oak, an immense tree beneath whose branches one Daniel Day used to invite his friends to feast with him on beans and bacon on the first Friday in July. In course of time great crowds were attracted, but Day never failed in his hospitality, distributing his stores from the hollow trunk of the oak. About 1725 a regular annual fair was established. Day had his coffin made of one of the limbs of this tree, which was blown off by a storm ; and dying in 1767, at the age of eighty-four, he was buried in it in Barking churchyard. The sole remaining fragment of Hainault Forest is to be found at Lambourne End ; but it is a

East Horndon. —All Saints Church

Shenfield — The Church of St Mary the Virgin.

beautiful fragment, where, as Sir Walter Besant says, there are "hillsides clothed with wood; slopes, on which, as you stand upon them and look among the trees, the sun produces strange and wonderful effects ; stretches of elastic turf ; great trees, avenues of oaks, gatherings of beeches, with ash, and elm, and sycamore ; everywhere the freshness and fragrance of the wild wood."

The village which bears the beautiful old name of Havering-atte-Bower stood formerly within the forest. It was the chosen retreat of that pious but rather feeble prince, Edward the Confessor. His character seems to be well pourtrayed in the otherwise absurd story which connects him with the place. The nightingales sang so loud that they disturbed his midnight devotions, and in answer to his prayer that this affliction might cease, the nightingales have been silent in the woody solitudes of Havering ever since. The spot continued to be a favourite retreat during subsequent reigns, and a palace which sheltered many royal personages stood here until the time of the Commonwealth. Havering until lately was a " liberty, " having its own magistrates and sessions. But the local offenders against the law, if any there be, stand no longer in awe of the ancient stocks, which are still an object of interest upon the shady village green. The place stands high, commanding a beautiful view to the south and east over the fertile Essex country and the winding Thames, while away to the west the forest appears as a dense mass of blackish-green.

Another fragment of the ancient forest is to be found much nearer London, at Wanstead Park, close to Forest Gate, where in earlier times a way into the wood branched off from the great high road to Colchester. Rising above the Roding, which still forms its eastern boundary, this little wilderness of two hundred acres was enclosed early in the eighteenth century by the first Earl Tilney, and a magnificent mansion was built upon the site. A hundred years later, a spendthrift who had married the sole heiress of the Tilney family brought everything under the hammer, and the house was demolished. Its grounds now form a public park of a wild beauty very rare in such places . As one traverses the pleasant paths that wind in all directions among the groves of forest trees, the eye is delighted by glimpses of water, where the Roding is spread out into lakes, and of small islands that are the haunt of herons.

To reach Epping Foprest from this point we follow the road northward ; and as the ground rises, and the fields and pastures beyond the Roding unroll before us, the red-brick tower of Woodford church comes into view. Just within the churchyard gate is a large stone tomb to William Morris of Woodford Hall, the father of the poet. The latter, one of the greatest of modern Englishmen, was born at Walthamstow,

but it was here that much of his boyhood and
youth was spent. The Hall, a large mansion of
Georgian date, adjoined the church, and was
only pulled down the other day. In Morris's
time the village pound and stocks stood just
across the road upon a bit of wayside green.
The park of fifty acres in which the mansion
stood was separated only by a fence from the
open forest behind. Morris himself said that
as a boy he knew the forest " yard by yard
from Wanstead to the Theydons, and from Hale
End to the Fairlop Oak ; it was always interesting and often very beautiful. " It is worth noting
how deeply this familiar landscape entered into
the mind of a man who, more than any other, has
re-created for us the romantic past. His bio-
grapher tells us that " he never ceased to love
Epping Forest, and to uphold the scenery of his
native county as beautifully and characteristically
English. The dense hornbeam thickets, which
even in bright weather have something of solem-
nity and mystery in their deep shade, and which
are hardly found elsewhere in England, reappear
again and again in his poetry and his prose
romances. " This is Morris's own description of
the forest: " The special character of it was
derived from the fact that by far the greater
part was a wood of hornbeams, a tree not common save in Essex and Herts. It was certainly
the biggest hornbeam wood in these islands, and

I suppose in the world. Nothing could be more interesting and romantic than the effect of the long poles of the hornbeams rising from the trunks and seen against the mass of the wood behind. it has a peculiar charm of its own not to be found in any other forest."

But no longer, alas! can we find at Woodford those pathless glades and thickets which still, as Mr Mackail says, "remain in all essentials a part of primeval England, little changed in the course of hundreds, perhaps thousands of years." To find these we must go still further north, towards Loughton and Theydon Bois. And here, more than anywhere, if we wish to find the real beauty and charm of the district, we must get off the beaten track. This is easy enough, as there are green rides and grasssy paths in all directions. More than once, on cloudy days, I have found myself quite lost among the trees, without the least notion of the points of the compass. But nowhere is it a gloomy forest, owing perhaps to the marked absence of pines and firs; in fact, the woodland is thoroughly English. The paths take one up and down steep declivities, through swampy hollows, across little streamlets running silently over beds of decaying leaves. In the seasons when the forest is least frequented it is also the most beautiful. In spring the different greens of the various trees are wonderfully striking, from a point such as High Beech where a wide stretch of woodland can be seen. Even when the skies are dark with gathering snow a wonderful picture is presented by the wooded ridges, the nearer ones blended into a mass of sepia contrasting with the opal blue of the more distant. But the forest in autumn is most wonderful of all when the russet and gold of the trees are bathed in the calm sunshine of Indian summer; the hillsides are clothed with purple heather, or with glowing masses of copper-coloured bracken; and the vivid green grass is sprinkled with fallen leaves of the brightest scarlet.

It is amid such surroundings as these that we come upon the famous Ambresbury Banks, which tradition points out as the scene of the struggle between Boadicea and Suetonius, but which at all events is a camp of very early origin. The ancient earthworks are still quite distinct, although imperfect and much obscured by trees. Standing upon the top of the rampart, one may hear the cooing of the wood-pigeons, watch the rabbits scampering in and out of their warrens, or perhaps catch a glimpse of the fallow deer whose progenitors were brought here by the countrymen of Suetonius. And close by runs the great white road to Cambridge, with a noise of continual traffic, including that of the motor-car.

Memories of the Abbey of Waltham are recalled by the beautiful Monk's Wood. Here among the solemn groves of beeches, upon an

autumn evening the stillness is complete.   Seen
through the trees is a landscape of perfect beauty.
And to think that this lovely forest was not long
ago continually preyed upon by the builder, and
being cut up into private pleasure-grounds for
successful business men !   One can but rejoice
that so much at least is left, and secured to the
free use of the people of London for ever.   For
this the City has deserved our gratitude.   Perhaps its action was unconsciously inspired by the
sentiment which bound the citizens to the forest
for so many generations, finding expression in
the beautiful custom of Maying, as described by
Stow.   In May the streets of old London are
said by him to have looked like bowers, from
the boughs of hawthorn or May which each
man hung over his doorway.   The young men
and maidens went a-maying after midnight, accompanied by bands of music.   They went " into
the sweet meadows and green woods, there to
rejoice their spirits with the beauty and savour
of sweet flowers, and with the harmony of birds,
praising God after their kind. "   They returned
at sunrise in joyful procession, carrying large
boughs of hawthorn, birch, and other trees,
garlanded with wreaths of wild flowers, and
bearing large nosegays in their hands, with
which they adorned the windows and doors of
their houses.   Thus it was to some extent
a people's forest in early times.   Even the

jealously-guarded rights of the chase were surrendered by the soverign at Easter, when the mayor, aldermen, and citizens of London were privileged to hunt within twenty miles of their city ; and this custom, known as the Epping Hunt, lasted in a more or less degenerate form until the Victorian era. And it is recorded how Edward the Fourth, who always sought the friendship of Londoners, invited the principal citizens to hunt with him in Waltham Forest ; a feast was spread for them under a canopy of green boughs, and the courteous monarch refused to sit until he saw his guests served.

But if the city has saved the forest from actual destruction, one must sorrowfully admit that it has almost ruined the lower end of it with improvements, which include an artificial lake and a huge hotel. It is not this pinchbeck paradise, but the virgin loveliness of Monk's Wood and Ambresbury Banks that makes a modern writer of refined taste call even the New Forest commonplace in comparison. Chingford must be passed over by the traveller who wishes to feel and retain the impression of Epping Forest as a romantic solitude. Let him linger among the trees on the higher ground until the hush of evening falls, and depart eastward into the quiet valley of the Roding as the white mists rise in the darkening hollows under the pale gleam of the moonrise

XXI

The Weald of Essex : Some Timber Churches

" There, morn to eve, the sunlight falls
On shingled spires, on gable walls,
On sloping pastures, wheatfields wide,
And woods where shy wild creatures hide. "

WHY not the Weald of Essex ? This word — the
Anglo-Saxon form of the Teutonic *Wald*, a forest,
— has come now to mean a richly-wooded country.
Such a district lies around what is left of the
actual forest. It is divided into fields and meadows,
and sprinkled with villages and farms ; yet it seems
to be still half woodland, and was at one time
wholly so. Look at the place-names of the district : Brentwood, probably the scene of a forest
fire, anciently sometimes written and still often pronounced *Burntwood* ; South Weald (there is a
North Weald near Epping), Greenstead, Doddinghurst, and so forth.

In Essex as a whole, but in this part of it more
especially, while timber is abundant, stone is scarce.
In early times the cost and labour of transporting
stone for building must have been very great, and
it was only natural that free use should be made

of another material which lay ready to hand. Hence we find that timber entered very largely into the construction of houses and even of churches.

And another substitute for stone — brick or tile — has been introduced by the Romans. Its use never entirely died out, but underwent a great revival in the fifteenth and sixteenth centuries. What the builders of that age were able to do with that material may still be seen in the splendid manor-houses which have come down to us more or less entire.

Ingatestone will make a very good starting-point for the district we are about to explore. This is the centre of the hundred square miles of Essex which was devastated in a quarter of an hour by a hailstorm on that black Midsummer Day of 1897. When I passed through it at harvest-time in that same year, the crops seemed to have been cut off a few inches above the ground, though no harvest had been reaped. Under the name of Audley Court, in her famous novel, "Lady Audley's Secret, " Miss Braddon gives a rather fanciful but on the whole an apt desription of Ingatestone Hall. This house was built in 1565 by Sir William Petre, a wily counsellor of Henry the Eighth, who had bought the manor at the Dissolution. It lies embowered in trees amidst quiet pastures. Entering beneath a turreted gate-way bearing an old clock and the inscription *Sans*

Dieu rien, you approach the long three-sided mellow-toned building, with its quaint turrets, gables, and chimneys. You do not find the traces of Saxon and Norman work of which the novelist speaks, but there is certainly the priest's hiding-chamber, and the lime-walk also is a reality ; indeed it is a weird enough place at twilight, when the leaves shiver in the gloom overhead and the shadows play on the surface of the weedy fish-pond at the edge of the path. The Hall is now occupied by several Roman Catholic families, and is no longer inhabited by the Petres. The tombs of Sir William Petre and of his son, the first Lord Petre, are to be seen in Ingatestone church, not half a mile away. Following a quiet lane through an avenue and rookery, you reach the high road, and the little town of Ingatestone lies before you. The warm roofs of its single street are picturesquely grouped, and from the midst of them rises the handsome church tower, which is of brick, like the Hall, and of the same date, though the body of the church is much older. More than half of the town is in the parish of Fryerning. Now Fryerning village stands on a neighbouring hill, and has a church of its own with another red-brick tower, buttressed and battlemented, even finer than that of Ingatestone, and forming a conspicuous landmark for miles around. This tower is attached to a simple nave and chancel, with Norman walls three feet in thickness, showing abundance of Roman tile. It is pleasant on a summer's day to sit in the cool porch under the shadow of old yews, and look across to the hills over the valley through which runs the Roman and modern high road. Further south along this road is Mountnessing, with a little lonely church two miles away on the other side. Close by the church stands the Hall, and in front of it a broad wooden bridge crosses the little river Wid that runs here through the meadows. The church itself, an Early English building originally, has a heavy west front of brick, dated 1653. Five miles south as the crow flies is a church entirely of brick, that of East Horndon, which is beautifully placed on a knoll surrounded by trees, but is now ruinous and no longer used for worship. It has curious priests' rooms over transept-like aisles, and in an altar tomb the heart of Anne Boleyn is said to have been deposited. North of East Horndon, on the road to Brentwood, we come to the pretty hamlet of Herongate, facing the tall rookery of Thorndon Park, the modern seat of the Petre family. From hence a road to the right leads to Billericay. This name ʼhas sorely puzzled those curious in such matters. The town with a broad street of old houses and shops, stands on high ground. It was a Roman station, and here, during the Peasant Revolt in the fourteenth century, the Essex men made a second abortive stand. Ecclesiastically, it was in mediæval times in the parish of Great Burstead, now a little hamlet with a fine but decaying church facing the Langdon hills, and for a long time Billericay had no church of its own, while even to-day its church is strictly speaking a chapel. This building, which stands half-way down the High Street, has an Early Perpendicular brick-work tower. In the tracery of the tower window, one can but admire the skill with which the detail usually carved in stone is worked out in moulded brick ; yet one feels that it is after all but a *tour de force.*

A far more characteristic feature of church building in the Essex weald is the use of timber — not only in the wood-work of roofs and in carved screens, but to a greater or less extent in the actual fabric of the church, and more especially in the tower or spire. To me there is something inexpressibly beautiful and affecting in these homely structures. Their builders had no quarries whence stone could be obtained, so they took such material as came into their hands, and wrought with the best skill they had an enduring framework of mighty beams. When this had been tenoned and mortised together, and surmounted by a spire protected by shingled boards, to make known from a distance that here stood the house of prayer, it barely rose above the surrounding trees from which it had been hewn. Thus it happens that you often come upon such a little unobtrusive building quite unexpectedly : a turn in the road, an opening in the foliage, — and a shaft of light reveals the delicate silver-grey of the spire.

At Shenfield a peculiarly slender, almost needle-shaped spire is upheld by massive timbers ; immense baulks of wood laid flat to form a foundation, with huge uprights joined by horizontal beams buttressed and braced by others set slant-wise, forming pointed arches, and the whole construction boldly displayed to view from the interior. But at Shenfield the slender clustered pillars and depressed arches that divide the nave from the single aisle are also of wood — an almost unique feature ; and this with the panelled roof of nave and chancel gives the whole interior an effect peculiarly rich and warm. When I first visited Shenfield church, the sexton was carefully polishing the carved wooden pillars, a labour intended by him as a kind of thank-offering, not only for recovery from a recent sickness, but also for the regular payment of his wages during the time he had been ill. He pointed with pride also to the well-swept paths, shaven grass-plots, and blooming roses in the churchyard. Hard by the church is Shenfield Hall, an ancient farmhouse of many gables, past which descends a shady lane that winds far into the sunlit weald

Three or four miles north-east is Mountnessing church, whose heavy brick front I mentioned just

now : I return to it again to note the timbers of
the tower, which stretch right into the nave and
even through the pews.   In one corner stands
an enormous old chest, hollowed out of a solid
block of wood ; the lid alone is almost too heavy
for one to lift.

Returning to the Chelmsford road, and passing
through Ingatestone, one sees, a mile or two
beyond the town, a stile and footpath on the
right-hand side leading to a little church not a
quarter of a mile away.   This lies immediately
beyond the main railway line, and is reached by
a level crossing :   the signal-post stand almost in
the rectory garden.   This is Margaretting.   The
lower part of the wooden tower is very spacious,
with a carved western doorway, and has a tiled
roof, from the midst of which rises a shingled
spire.   There is a north porch of dark timber (not
nearly so beautiful as that at Benfleet, but still
very handsome), elaborately carved with quatrefoil
and other ornament.   Entering by it, one notes
the open oak roof and carved chancel screen.
Pushing aside a heavy curtain that hangs in the
tower archway, one finds again the splendid construction of the timber tower, and sees that the
walls are filled in with plaster between the outer
upright beams.   On the floor of the tower is
a slab to the memory of a man and his wife, who
died within ten months of each other, with this
curious verse upon it:

" Shee on this clayen pillow laid her head,
  As Brides doe vse, the first to go to bed.
  He mist her soon, and yet ten months, he trys
  To live apart, but liks it not, and dys."

From Margaretting a rough road eastward leads
over the pretty river Wid and ascends past charming copses until at length it turns into a farmyard.
Here I encountered a lad who was ingeniously
propelling himself in a wheelbarrow, and asked
him the way to Stock. " Follow the telegrams, "
was his reply, which I understood better when I
saw a line of telegraph posts and wires stretching
across the upland country, through ploughed fields
and pastures. A rough cart-track ran beside
it, which brought me at length to the village,
which is a large and ancient one, and stands high.
The church stands on the western edge of the
hill, and is interesting when seen directly after
that of Margaretting, as the wooden tower is very
similar in design. The western doorway is a good
one, with carved arcading, and quatrefoil ornament above it, and the tower windows with
mullions and tracery wrought in timber are very
handsome ; but the wood has warped and split in
places, proving that it is after all, in the exterior
of buildings, but a makeshift for stone.

Leaving the village, the westward road goes
down a sandy declivity with patches of furze,
and pursues a quiet course until the church of
Buttsbury is reached ; a plain building ruined by

successive alterations, but beautifully situated, overlooking the meadows of the Wid, with Ingatestone Hall near at hand among the trees, and the old church and town in the distance. Following a path through the meadows the town is reached, the high road crossed, and the way continued up the wooded hills upon the further side.

Embosomed in woods lies the quiet village of Blackmore. Here the church has an almost perfect Norman west end in conjunction with a timber tower. This tower is so similar to that at Margaretting that it is thought likely that they were built by the same architect, especially as both churches belonged to Blackmore priory. The priory, of which nothing now remains, owned the manor-house adjoining the church, which bears the curious name of Jericho, while a a stream that runs near is called the Jordan. These names are said to have originated at the Court of Henry the Eighth, whose courtiers were wont to say, when he disappeared in pursuit of his amorous intrigues, that the king had " gone to Jericho. " Here he spent much of his time with the witty and beautiful Elizabeth Taillebois, who in 1519 bore him a son, named by him Henry Fitzroy. The king was passionately attached to the boy, and created him Earl of Nottingham, Duke of Richmond and Somerset, and Knight of the Garter, at the age of six ; at eight he was made Admiral of England,

Blackmore — The Church of St Laurence.

Blackmore — Jericho Priory

Ireland and Normandy. He was married to Mary, daughter of the Duke of Norfolk, but died, to Henry's intense grief, when only seventeen years of age.

From Blackmore it is but an easy walk to Doddinghurst. The church here has a very fine and unusually long porch of dark timber, which has lost something of its antique look by recent restoration. Beneath the porch is a charming Early English doorway, and to the same period belong the three splayed lancets that dimly illuminate the chancel. Over the rood beam are carved and coloured figures of the Saviour on the cross, the Virgin and the Apostle John, which though perhaps not ancient, harmonise perfectly with their surroundings. There is a fine open timber roof, the joints of which are secured by wooden pins projecting about an inch on each side. There is also a wooden tower of the same pattern as the others that have been mentioned, and here also the construction is frankly shown, though I was told that a recent visitor said that the tower wanted an arch to hide the timber ! Close to the churchyard is an old house, hardly more than a cottage, with a detached ivied chimney. It is now the home of the village schoolmaster, but in pre-Reformation days was the presbytery, or priests' house. The most famous example of this kind of dwelling is at Alfriston in Sussex; we have seen another at Ashdon ; while there is a house under the shadow of the church at Runwell, near Wickford, which probably had the same origin ;   at all events the tie beams and king-posts that support the roof in the upper chambers are of exactly the same construction as those in the church.   To return to Dodding-hurst.   I noticed a number of the villagers wait-ing in groups near the churchyard gate, and presently discovered the reason ;   a wedding pro-cession on foot came up the rural road in the spring sunshine.   Walking by himself was the sexton, ostentatiously swinging the key that marked his office ;   a few yards behind came three couples of young men and maidens in their best clothes — the foremost man, evidently the bride-groom, having a wooden leg.   I did not stay to hear any of the marriage service beyond a pro-hibition of the throwing of confetti and rice in the sacred precincts.   In a field hard by the church two men were sowing oats by hand, with a rhythmic swing of the body, out of shallow wooden baskets.   One of them passing near the hedge stopped for a moment's chat.   It was an old-fashioned way of scattering the seed, he said, but it needed a lot of learning.   I remarked that it was at all events a scriptural custom.   " Yes, they didn't have no machinery in them days. " Then he gave me his views on modern agri-culture.   " The farmers let the land get out of order, won't do anything to it, and than grumble at bad seasons. " Not far off, however, in spite of bad seasons, a windmill was busily at work. The sign of the *White Swan* rose out of a little island in the midst of a pond, with a bunch of palm growing around the sign-post. Beyond the wind-mill, long poles and faggot-stacks, piled up in the most orderly fashion, proclaimed the where-abouts of a woodman. In this part of Essex these men obtain a lease for felling wood of a certain size at so much an acre. Within this parish are the village stocks, and another relic of old-world punishments, a whipping-post. The latter, which also serves as a guide-post stands on a piece of grass at a cross-road, and has on each of two sides a species of iron handcuffs, which when padlocked down would hold an un-fortunate prisoner firmly by the wrists. The guide post points to Ongar.

At Ongar the Roding runs through the meadows, and from the bridge that spans it a single street of quaint houses rises to the top of the hill, where stands the church, and behind it, screened in trees, what remains of the moats and the castle mound. A portion of the town actually stands within the limits of the ancient castle built by the famous De Lucy, who obtained for the place its market, and incidentally its name of Chipping Ongar. De Lucy, " the loyal, " as his king called him, rendered his royal master valuable service ; to please him he persuaded the monks to appoint Becket archbishop of Canterbury; he presided at the council of Clarendon, for which Becket never forgave him, and he was as powerful with his sword as with his tongue. At last he retired to a monastery in Kent, and died there. De Lucy may possibly have built the church at Ongar. Here, in cutting away the plaster to expose the original wall of flint and Roman tile, a strange round-arched recess was discovered, communicting with the interior of a church by a small window — probably a penance chamber or a hermit's cell.

Quite near to the town is Greenstead, as is implied by its legal title of Greenstead-juxta-Ongar. A walk of no more than a mile across the fields brings one to this leafy spot, which holds a church of strange and romantic interest. It looks a neat and trim little church now, since restorations have several times been carried out, but its famous wooden walls seem to remain substantially as they were built. They are formed of oak or chestnut trees, says a modern and very exact writer, " not, as usually described, half trees, since they have had a portion of the centre or heart cut out, probably to furnish beams for the construction of the roofs and sills. The outside or slabs, thus left, were placed on the sill, but by what kind of tenon they are there retained does not appear ; while the upper ends, being roughly adzed off to a thin edge, are let into a groove, which, with the piece of timber in which it is cut, runs the whole length of the building itself. The door-posts are of squared timber, and are secured in the grooves by small wooden pins, still firm and strong — a truly wonderful example of the durability of British oak. . . . The outsides of all the trees are furrowed to the depth of about an inch into long, stringy ridges, by the decay of the softer parts of the timber; but these ridges seem equally hard as the heart of the wood itself. " Who does not know the story which tradition attaches to this ancient church? King Edmund the Martyr, tied to a tree and shot with arrows by the Danes in the year 870, A.D., was buried in East Anglia where he died. His body was afterwards brought to London for safety; but in 1013 it was decided to restore it to St Edmund's Bury. On its way into Suffolk, the body rested for a night at Greenstead. One tradition tells us that the wooden church commerorates this event; another, that it is the original shrine erected to receive the body. Why should not both accounts be true? Our ancestors in a semi-barbarous epoch, to shelter the body of this royal saint for perhaps a single night, built a temporary resting-place which serves as a permanent place of worship for after generations. Surely we shall recall with affectionate reverence the honest enduring labour of those old-time craftsmen, as well as the procession of chanting priests and the torches around the dead king's bier.

XXII

The Weald of Essex: Brentwood

"Old, unhappy, far-off things."

BRENTWOOD stands in the midst of the weald country on the great Roman and modern road to East Anglia ; and whether you approach it by this road or by any other you have to climb a hill. Its long straight High Street, notwithstanding many modern changes, still presents a succession of old-fashioned houses and shops, and here and there one with pointed gables. Looking under archways and down alleys as you pass along the street, you get glimpses of old stabling and out-houses. In the centre of the town, just past the town-hall, whose clock hangs across the street, you see a fine old-fashioned smithy in full activity ; and close by are two of the many coaching inns which remain. In the perspective of the street the more picturesque of the two is undoubtedly the *George and Dragon*, which, standing at the corner of Crown Street, shows its timbered, well-propotioned walls, its chimneys and tiled roofs, to great advantage. But the inn over the way is much older, al-

214

though the plain brick front added in recent years rather conceals the fact. The *White Hart*, with gilded antlers, hangs couchant above a wide archway, on the side of which is a notice that the inn was established in 1480. Passing through, and observing the black timber framework of the walls, you reach the splendid galleried courtyard ; or rather what is left of it, for the right hand portion no longer exists ; but enough remains to make a charming picture, and to suggest the former beauty of the whole. Skirting the array of barrels which is always piled against the wall, and going past the ostlers' quarters, you go through another archway and reach a second courtyard surrounded by stables and outbuildings of great extent, all of dark timber, the prevailing feature of which is the depressed arch. Beyond are the gardens and the bowling-green, and a lane that leads to South Weald. Perhaps you may meet the old cattle-dealer who can tell you tales of the coaching-days before the railway came to Brentwood, and who has often ridden as a postillion in and out of this very yard, when a former landlord drove four-in-hand with a flower in his button-hole.

Notwithstanding the former importance of Brentwood as a coaching stage, and as a market and assize town, it was ecclesiastically only a hamlet of South Weald, which manor was granted to Waltham Abbey by Edward the Confessor and Harold. After the Conquest it passed into the hands of the monks of St Osyth's priory, who in 1221 founded here a chapel in honour of Thomas à Becket, which accounts for the dedication to St Thomas the Martyr of the modern church which has replaced the ancient chapel and stands near its site. The reverence in which " this turbulent priest " was held everywhere after his death must surely have been due to some greatness of character as well as to the tragic circumstances of his end. The chapel was visited by streams of people from the neighbouring counties. Pilgrim's Hatch (a name which, like the archaic spelling of Havering-atte-Bower, recalls the England of Chaucer) is a spot two miles from Brentwood on the Ongar road, where the pilgrims to the chapel passed through a gate into or out of the forest. The chapel stood on the south side of the High Street, and there, under the spire of the new church, may be seen the sole remains of it — a portion of the tower. The ground in which it stands looks like a private garden, but is really an open space belonging to the church. A mass of ruined masonry, covered wiith ivy, is sustained by tall pointed arches, enclosing a space which once formed the base of the tower ; in one angle is a newel staircase. This old place derives its interest not only from the pilgrimages formerly made to it, but from the story which connects it with Hubert de Burgh. Incurring the king's displeasure, this royal favourite took refuge here ; but his ruthless enemies violated the sanctuary and dragged him forth. A smith was ordered to shackle him, but replied that he would die any death rather than fetter the man who saved England from the stranger On the remonstrance of the Bishop of London, Hubert was replaced in sanctuary, but a strong guard was set round the chapel, and he was starved out. On his surrendering, he was sent to the Tower, and though eventually released he never regained his power in the realm.

Round Brentwood spreads a landscape of indescribable beauty and delicacy. From the footpath to Shenfield, which runs parallel with the high road, the wooded hills to the north can be seen for miles, one low range withdrawn beyond another. Shenfield, whose church we have already visited is taking on a new aspect since the railway junction was made, but along the broad road that descends between the trees from Brentwood the tale of a former day is still told by a few old houses and inns. Here at night the only sign of life beyond the lights in the inn-parlours is the string of haycarts on their way to London for the early market. The fragrant load is piled well forward over the shafts and balanced by a corresponding weight overhanging behind ; the horses steam in the light of the lanterns as thay plod along the road, guided mainly by their own intelligence, while the weary carter, who may have been at work since daybreak, is perhaps unconsciously qualifying for an appearance before the magistrate on a charge of "riding asleep."

South of the high road is Shenfield Common, which is practically a part of Brentwood, and over which may be seen among the trees the immense white frontage of Thorndon Hall, the almost deserted seat of the Petre family. Beyond the common with its sandy banks of furze interspersed with ponds, and across the deep railway cutting, is Warley Gap, whence may be obtained a glorious view over the Thames to the Kentish uplands. The great mass of wooded hill that rises to the east is the Langdon range, but for which we should be able from this point to see Hubert de Burgh's castle of Hadleigh.

Looking westward from Brentwood down the London road, the ground falls steeply towards the Weald Brook, and its small tributary streams, which, marked by pollard trees, and cutting deep into the soft loamy banks, divide the meadows with fantastic curves and loops. Where the Weald Brook runs beneath the road is Brook Street. Here formerly stood a leper hospital; and here still stands, among other pleasant old houses, an inn with the pictorial sign of the *Golden Fleece*, spacious and quaint, but fallen upon evil days. From here a quiet lane gently ascends to the village of South Weald; or it may be reached by another from the top of the hill at Brentwood.

Seated upon a swelling slope amid green pasture and dark woodland, the grey stone tower of South Weald church with its corner turret is at all times a feature of the landscape on which the eye rests with pleasure, especially when in the morning sunshine, as I have sometimes seen it, it glows softly like a gem. The road from Brentwood dips into the valley, and as it rises again, between over-arching trees, you look back and see the town with its tiled roofs and walled gardens spread along the ridge, surrounded by elms and poplars, and surmounted by its modern but not ungraceful spire. Continuing up the hill, you reach upon the right hand a beautiful undulating park, with bracken, soft turf, fine timber, and herds of deer. The road widens into three terraces, from the topmost of which you can see far into the park on the one side, and over fields and spinneys on the other. The trees grow denser, and are thronged with rooks ; presently the church is seen close at hand, its tower of Kentish ragstone contrasting with walls of flint in which are perpendicular windows. The churchyard, which is beautifully kept, is paved with old carved and lettered tombstones, leading to the wide wooden porch, where it is pleasant to rest awhile. Within the porch is a Norman doorway, the relic of an earlier church, showing zig-zag mouldings on its arch and columns, and having a chequered tympanum. The spot is exquisitly peaceful. Passing out by another paved path set with rose-trees, and through the timber lych-gate, the quaint cottage which serves as a post-office stands in a sheltered corner on the right, the smoke that rises from its chimneys showing blue against the trees behind. A shady avenue of limes leads downhill to where a lake lies on either side of the road, connected by a stream that runs beneath it ;   swans float upon the surface of the lakes, or preen their dazzling white feathers on the sunny bank. Within the park, and partly screened from the road by thick hedges is Weald Hall, a modernised Tudor house. Here the unhappy Princess Mary lived before she came to the throne ;   and during her reign it became the seat of Sir Anthony Browne, Chief Justice of Common Pleas, who died in 1567, as may be seen from an inscription on his tomb in the church. This Browne seems to have been a typical time-serving courtier of the Tudor age, yet he must have had his good points, for he founded the almshouses which may still be seen in this parish, and the grammar-school in Brentwood, whither we must retrace our steps to follow his history further. If we return round the park, turning as we do so to the left, and passing the remains of an ancient — possibly British — camp, we shall reach Pilgrim's Hatch, where it will be noticed that several green lanes meet. There are one or two old inns, and a curious post-office in the side of a farmhouse.

We are now on the road from Ongar to Brentwood, a beautifully wooded one still, and within recent years very thickly timbered indeed. Where this road enters Brentwood, at the top of the High Street, stands a granite obelisk in memory of William Hunter, burned as a heretic in March 1555. Not many yards away stands the Martyr's Oak, an exceedingly old tree-trunk, fast falling to decay, and with its hollows bricked up; near or beneath this tree it was that Hunter suffered. The old red-brick building close by, with diamond-paned mullioned windows, is the grammar-school founded by Sir Anthony Browne in 1557. Now this was two years later than the burning of Hunter, in which Browne took no small share. Did he really think that he was doing God service?

A full account of Hunter's case is to be found in Foxe's "Book of Martyrs." Foxe is a violent partisan, but historians tell us he is to be trusted when he says that he obtained his knowledge from actual witnesses of the scenes he describes. Now Foxe says that he had his account from Robert Hunter, the brother of William; and his story is full of 'human touches, illustrating what he describes as "nature striving with religion." William Hunter then, in the first year of Queen Mary, was in his nineteenth year, and apprentice to a silk-weaver in Coleman Street, London. Being commanded at Easter to attend mass, he refused, and was threatened with punishment ; whereupon his master, foreseeing trouble, required him to depart, and William came to his father at Brentwood, remaining with him some weeks. Going one day into the chapel (whose remains we have seen), and finding a Bible, he began to read. Father Attwell, hearing him, came to him, and said, " What ! meddlest thou with the Bible ? " He added, what has indeed proved true, though his assumption of cause and effect may be doubted, " It was never Merrie England since the Bible came abroad in English. " Finding he could make nothing of Hunter, he promised to bring one who should be able to deal with him, and fetched the " Vicar of Southwell. " (Note here that Brentwood was merely a hamlet of South Weald, to which parish the chapelry was always subordinate. " The officiating chapel priest had to swear that he would do the mother parish no harm. He paid tribute, two pounds of wax, yearly to the South Weald parson. He baptised no one, he buried no one; nor might he offer communion or receive confession on Sundays or other holidays without the parson's leave, except on the day of St Thomas's passion or translation, and at the time of the fair. " For twenty years the chapel was without a priest, as appears from a record in the Brentwood vestry-books of an action brought against a descendant of Sir Anthony Browne, who had neglected to provide one). The vicar of South Weald came and conversed with Hunter, but failed to shake him, and had recourse to threats, so that Hunter fled. The vicar thereupon reported the matter to " Master Browne, " who sent for the constable and for Hunter's father. The father, being threatened with imprisonment unless he delivered up his son, said, " Would you have me seek out my son to be burned ? " However, he went two or three day's journey, and by chance, as we are asked to believe, met William, who came home with him. When Browne had Hunter brought before him, he tried his hand at theological controversy, but with small success. It must be admitted that Hunter, though sincere and brave, seems to have lacked somewhat both of Christian charity and of the respect due to an older man ; and Browne could hardly be expected to forgive the taunt that he himself, no doubt in an earlier reign, had spoken against the Mass. Hunter was sent to Bishop Bonner, who put him in the stocks in the gate-house with bread and water ; and as he refused to touch this food, he was laid in irons. After an imprisonment lasting three-quarters of a year, he was, on 9th of February, formally condemned. Bonner is entitled to credit for one last effort to save him from his fate : " If thou wilt yet recant, I will make thee a freeman in the city, and give thee forty pounds in good money to set up thy trade with. Or I will make thee steward of my house, and set thee in office, for I like thee well ; thou hast wit enough, and I will prefer thee, if thou recant. "   After another month in Newgate, Hunter was sent to Brentwood on the Saturday before the Annunciation of the Blessed Virgin ; but he remained in custody until the day after, because of the holiness of that day.   His mother came to see him, and told him that she was glad she was so happy as to bear such a child : " Yea, I think thee as well bestowed as any child that ever I bare. "   On the morning after Lady-Day, the sheriff set forward the burning.   The sheriff's son came to see William in the prison to prepare him, and tried to comfort him, till he could speak no more to him for weeping.   The dreadful procession started from the *Swan Inn* (still standing at the lower end of the High Street), and reached the place of execution.   " Master Brown " was in attendance, and declared " here is not wood enough to burn a leg of him "   William exclaimed, " Son of God, shine upon me ! "   and immediately the sun in his element shone out of a dark cloud so full in his face that he was constrained to look another way.   He flung his psalter into the hand of his brother, who said, " William, think on the holy passion of Christ, and be not afraid. "   He answered, " I am not afraid.   Lord, receive my spirit ! "   and casting down his head into the smothering smoke, he yielded up his life for the truth.

South Weald.

Doddinghurst — The Church of All Saints.

XXIII

By Lea and Stort

" Waving boughs and shaded streams
Fill the sylvan way with dreams. "— *C.Dalmon.*

HE would be a bold man that should venture to
write of the Lea after Izaak Walton.   The brim-
ming river, with its willows and buttercups, lives
in his pages for all time.   Yet I have a grievance
against the Compleat Angler.   To read him one
would think that the Lea was wholly in Hertford-
shire, because he " stretched his legs " mostly on
that side of the river ;   but a river has two banks,
and the other bank of the Lea belongs to Essex.
Speaking generally, the Lea, and its feeder the
Stort, form the western boundary of the county :
and near these streams some very beautiful but
little-visited country is to be found.

At Broxbourne, the angler's paradise, the pretty
little hostelry by the bridge stands on Essex soil.
The road eastward runs through a beautiful avenue
of poplars.   Presently the view widens, and before
you is a long green slope, at the summit of which
can be descried, about two miles away, the square
brick tower of Nazing Church.   Keeping along

P

the winding and gently ascending road, or taking a steeper and more direct path across the fields, you stand at length under the chestnut-trees by the churchyard gate, and are rewarded by the splendid prospect of forest scenery that greets you, with the Lea gleaming among the meadows in the valley.   Beyond the church, the road ends in a gate that opens on Nazing Common — a breezy stretch of undulating upland.

The day when I first went there happened to be Whit-Monday, and a " fair " was being held in a field attached to a tavern.   A woman stood ringing a large bell, after the fashion of a railway porter at a country station, outside a long barn with tarred wooden walls and a thatched roof. Expecting to find some sort of entertaining going on, I looked in, and was not disappointed.   The barn was full of villagers sitting round rough tables supported by trestles and laden with goodly joints and pyramids of steaming vege-tables :   and before the bell had ceased ringing everyone was in his place and the knives and forks in full activity.   It was a club dinner, and obviously a great function.   All present seemed in high good humour.   I caught one sample of rustic wit.   " Here, have a bit of this.   It's no good waiting till it's all gone, and then saying, I should have liked a bit of that. "   The dialect was Essex, not Wessex ;   but somehow I was reminded of Mr Thomas Hardy's peasants.   Not being a member of the club, I contented myself with a cold repast in the inn. Resuming my walk along shaded lanes and past pretty hamlets, I came to Potter Street, where is a fine common crossed by a splendid double avenue of elms. A mile of unavoidable high road, terminating in a hill, brought me to Harlow. No sooner had I passed the first two or three houses than the town ended, and there were the green fields beyond. I rubbed my eyes, and thought that Harlow must be further on. The one long street of which the town consists lies across, not along the modern high road. Perhaps in former times this road from north to south was less frequented than that which runs east and west. A quarter of a mile beyond the town, I found the gem of the place — the little Norman chapel, now used as a barn. It is most curious and picturesque, with its narrow splayed windows, its richly-decorated doorways, and firm walls mantled with ivy.

Turning westward, I followed a beautiful road, overlooking the valley of the Stort, to Netteswell Cross. This little hamlet stands, as its name suggests, at the junction of intersecting roads ; its exquisite *Greyhound Inn* and quaint cottages are charmingly grouped in a little green hollow, and should be a godsend to a painter in search of a subject.

Taking a tempting field-path, I came to Netteswell church, here, as so often in remote country places, a sort of adjunct to the manor-house. The cowherd who unlocked the church was eloquent concerning its antiquity, as is the manner of rustics ; but he had no more idea than rustics usually have which parts of the structure were really ancient. He pointed out to me in an awed whisper the grave of a man who " didn't believe in God almighty " ; but, so far as I could learn, the only ground for this assertion was that the deceased had not attended church.

From Netteswell the path led me across fields of scented pea-blossom, along a brook by the side of beautiful woods, and so at length to Great Parndon. In the tower of the church here, I found an arched outer doorway, without a door, leading to a spiral staircase. The stairs were so dark, and so worn by the feet of successive generations, that it was hard to climb them ; when I reached the top, moreover, a door barred further progress. Still, I could admire the beauty of construction whereby the inner corners of the wedge-shaped steps are rounded so as of themselves to form a central pillar, polished smooth by innumerable hands. The elegant solidity of this prevalent feature of mediæval buildings is to my mind beyond praise.

Gaining the road to Roydon, I noticed on the brow of a hill a pair of half timbered Tudor cottages, the dark wood of their flat-arched door-

ways and windows contrasting finely with the
white plaster of the walls. Hankering to see
one of the interiors, I found an excuse to knock.
The door opened into the living-room, wherin
lay a poor bed-ridden old woman. A young
neighbour had come in with her baby to cheer
the old dame up a little. She suffered constant
pain, and was dependent, I found, on the parish ;
yet the few words she spoke were full of the
serenity of a fervent religious faith. Strangely
enough, the lesson this brought home to me was
again enforced when a little later I came to another
Tudor building — the remains of Nether Hall.
Only a ruinous though beautiful tower gateway is
left of a stately mansion, once the home of the
Colte family, which gave a wife to Sir Thomas
More. Like this poor suffering woman of to-day,
that great and noble man, of whom his age was not
worthy,

> " Set up a mark of everlasting light
> Above the howling senses' ebb and flow. "

And is it not the epochs when reverence for the
unseen prevailed that awaken our reverence now ?

Another day, still keeping close to the county-
boundary, I travelled a northward road with the
Stort in full flood appearing now and again upon
the left hand. At length I came to the spot of
which I was in search — the ancient entrenchment
known as Walbury. I found it thickly covered

with trees, the growth of centuries ;   this is often
the case with these old earthworks, perhaps because of the obstacles offered to the plough by
the bank and ditch.   A great farm stands near
the ramparts, which overlook the meadows and
the river.   I made the circuit of the place along
the bottom of the trench, with the trees over-
arching it above and dead leaves lining it below.
When again I climbed the steep bank on the north
side, I saw a picture like one of Dürer's charming
backgrounds.   On a sloping hill, less than a mile
away, the old houses of a little village clustered
together, with substantial stacks in the surrounding fields, and the slender spire of a church at the
summit.   This was Little Hallingbury.   Great
Hallingbury, a mile or so further on, proved to be
an even smaller place, though with a larger church,
much restored, and a graveyard that seemed to tell
of a considerable population in former times.   The
rooks cawed among the trees surrounding the
towers of Hallingbury Place, whose high lawns
looked over the wooded river valley into Hertford-
shire.

Eastward of Hallingbury I skirted the edge of
Hatfield Forest, catching now and then a glimpse
of the deer that still haunt this now enclosed
wilderness.   Presently the swiftly-turning sails of
a windmill came into view on higher ground, and
I came to Hatfield Heath, a breezy common with
houses grouped around it.   The road descended

again, and presently crossed a little river. On the
steep green banks opposite rose a little town of
charming aspect, dominated by the embattled tower
of a church. The clerestory windows rose above
the low tiled or thatched roofs of the humble
white-washed houses in the quiet street through
which I passed. No traces remain of the priory,
which Aubrey de Vere founded here in the twelfth
century, and of which the church formed part; but
for its beautiful situation, and its architectural expression of a bygone age, Hatfield Broad Oak is
as characteristic an Essex town as one could wish
to see.

XXIV

Windmill Land: The Rodings

" And the windmill sails are turning, turning, turning. "

WEARY of perpetual prosaic disillusionment, the
soul of man turns wistfully back to ages of
myth. We begin, for example, to perceive a
meaning in the old idea that every river has an
individuality of its own. There is a certain
fascination, born of our instinct for continuity, in
tracing the shy and devious wanderings of some
favourite stream. Those who do not feel this will
never understand the charm of the little river
Roding, or find the clue to the sequestered country
through which it steals. Rising obscurely in the
sylvan recesses of Easton, and passing beneath the
great highway that traverses Essex east to west,
it is still hardly more than a brook when it stirs
the rushes round the base of Canfield Mount.
Through quiet meadows and woods it flows, still
southward, till it rounds the spur of the Epping
ridge at Ongar, and waters the wide valley which
spreads to the east of the forest ; beyond the
upland pastures of Lambourne with its little de-

serted Early Norman church; through Abridge village and under Passingford Bridge, and on till it is fouled by the stain of London and is lost at last in the Thames.

This little unfrequented river gives its name to a stretch of country about twelve miles long, lying between Ongar and Dunmow — a cluster of villages called " The Rodings, " bounded west and east by two lesser clusters, the Lavers and the Easters. Perhaps no part of Essex is so entirely remote from the life of modern London. The books dismiss the district as " almost wholly agricultural. " Vast fields of wheat, oats and barley, interspersed now and then with woods, are traversed by roads and lanes along which you may saunter for hours almost without meeting a human being. Across a restless expanse of corn you may see and keep in sight for a mile or more — gazing at you with an almost human look — the casements and gables of some great white solitary farmhouse, which, when at length you reach it, you find surrounded by a moat. The labouring arms of a windmill on the horizon show where a village is to be found ; for in the Rodings every village has its windmill, always in close proximity to the church. Indeed the villages usually consist of nothing but church and windmill, with perhaps two or three cottages and a farm. It is becoming rare now in England to see a windmill, and rarer to find one at work. Looking one day into a barn in one of the Roding parishes, I noticed a still stranger survival — the operation of thrashing with a flail. These things serve to show that this part of Essex, geographically near London though it be, is centuries behind and apart from it. For nearness to London is not to be measured by miles. There are many places a good deal further away from it on the map which are far more under its influence, and where you have, in the words of Jeffries, " a dim sense of something wanting . . . a restlessness, a feeling that it is essential to be moving. " Here, on the contrary, the magnetism of the city ceases to act, and the magnetism of the earth has full sway, giving one what Jefferies so longed for — " absolute quiet, peace and rest. "

Nor is there in this district any striking object of historic interest ; not a single old castle or abbey is to be found within its length and breadth. Some beautiful old moated manor-houses indeed there are, but these are not ruins, and are heeded as little as the rolling landscape of which they seem a part.

The isolation of this piece of country seems the more remarkable, as, besides the tangled lanes which connect its villages and hamlets, there is a good high road running through the district. For several miles it is quite level and perfectly straight ; it runs along rather elevated ground, and commands a wide prospect. One summer evening on which I passed along it still lives in my memory, especially the picture of a group of labourers, wearied with their long days work in the harvest-field, resting and refreshing themselves outside a humble inn. Before them stretched a wide valley, thrown into shadow by the setting sun, which yet shone brightly upon the tower of High Easter church two miles away, and showed the smoke rising straight into the still air. I was returning, I remember, from Great Cranfield, where I had been impressed not so much by the romantic beauty of the Mount, one of the ancient strongholds of the De Veres, as by the projecting workshop of the shoemaker's house. I had seen one just like it at Felstead, and another on the stage in *Die Meister-singer.* Hans Sachs himself got up from his bench and told me all he knew about the Mount and the church that stands near it ; then he got his little granddaughters to prepare tea for me, which they did with a good deal of mirth and excitement. Next morning I stood between the sister churches of Willingale Doe and Willingale Spain, while the level rays of the rising sun cast long shadows across the golden cornfileds and bathed the sylvan land-scape in almost ethereal light.

Very pleasant is the memory of a summer holi-day spent with my household in a farmhouse on the edge of this interesting district. At a point where the high road takes a sudden turn to the right, you may see a white gate, usually lying back against the hedge. This leads into a rough farm

road, which takes you past a coppice, until some
hundreds of yards further a white house comes in
sight, backed by dark woods and by low hills in
the distance. In front of it spreads an ample park-
like chase, its undulating surface shadowed here
and there by graceful clumps of chestnut and elm.
Following a faint track slant-wise across the grass,
you go through a little wicket and across a foot-
bridge, which leads you over a deep grassy ditch.
The latter, from its rectangular form, you perceive
to be the remains of the moat which formerly protected the house. The ample proportions of the
building are in keeping with its ancient dignity.
The house-door stands open, and reveals to you,
beyond the hall, which is paved with tiles and
panelled with dark polished oak from floor to
ceiling, a glimpse of sunlit garden beyond the
further bank of the moat. If you pass through,
and then glance up at the house, the old-world
aspect of the place is even more striking; for the
slightly cold and formal lines of the front have
given place to bold projecting gables and massive
chimney stacks. Nothing is more significant of
the mean artificial spirit of these latter centuries
than the way in which we try to hide away our
chimneys as something to be ashamed of. In these
northern latitudes the domestic fire is a prime
necessity of life. This fact was naïvely expressed
in the so-called barbarous epoch, when the house
consisted simply of a hall with the hearth in the

centre. In the Middle Ages, when architecture was still self-respecting, the same fact was frankly accepted, and the chimney was made the centre of construction, with the other parts of the dwelling clustered round it. The house of which I speak is still known by the name which belonged to its owner in the reign of Henry the Fourth. Its barns and outbuildings apparently date from the same period. One of them especially impressed me with its framework of enormous beams supporting an arched timber roof such as one sees in churches. There was no agricultural depression in those times.

Here we spent many happy days, sometimes taking our ease in the harvest-field, at others exploring the surrounding country, either on foot, or in company with an old pony, or in carriers' carts. In the hot August afternoons, while the cyclists whirred by along the dusty road, we would get over the stile into the fields, and rest on the shady green banks overhanging the river, where the boughs drooped low over the water, and dappled its surface with shadow. Much of the soil beneath the banks had been washed away, exposing the roots of the trees. Now and then a roach would slide out from the weeds and lie luxuriously in the sunlit water where it flowed pellucid over the gravel. He would perhaps allow your hand to come within a few inches of him, then suddenly dart several yards up stream like a flash of quicksilver.

Not until the cool of the evening, when the lights began to gleam across the darkening chase from the windows of the old house, and the dog barked his welcome at the sound of our footsteps, would we return to what we soon learned to regard as " home. "   As we fell asleep at night in an exquisitely fresh white room, we would hear the cry of the owl in the great barn, and be wakened in the morning by the plaintive cooing of wood-pigeons in the elms beyond the moat.   Such are the peaceful signs that mark the passage of the hours in an Essex farmhouse of the olden time.

XXV

Among the " Fields "

" A good land ; a land of brooks of water, of fountains and depths that spring out of valleys and hills ; a land of wheat and barley. "— Book of Deuteronomy.

THE smouldering sunset fades, and blends the distant trees confusedly together, as we drive along beneath the over-arching boughs. The wind is cold on this clear evening of late September, and we are glad to wrap ourselves in the rugs which the clear-eyed young carrier has provided. Next to him on the driver's seat is an old man, perhaps a shepherd, whose speech and countenance are kindly intelligent and full of character. Opposite to us are two merry country girls. Presently, at a crossroad, the waggonette stops ; they alight, and help to lift down a box too heavy for them to carry. This is laid on the three-cornered patch of grass which surrounds the white sign-post. They wish us good-night in a cheery tone, though the expected brother or sweetheart has clearly not yet arrived. Lamps are being lighted in the cottages as we reach Great Bardfield, and cross the bridge, over the river that reflects the swaying poplars. Through a low warm haze, a red moon rises over a wooded slope in the distance, crowned by a church tower which marks the end of our journey. A series of sharp turns, and we find ourselves again among houses, clustered irregularly round a wide green hollow, and enter an inn-yard surrounded by stables and outbuildings. Close above us appears the church, and the moon near it, now clear of the mist, shining brightly over the whole scene. A few hearty words of welcome from host and hostess, and, with the ready freemasonry of country inns, we are forthwith installed into the best that the house can bestow.

With the morning light we take in from our gable window a birds-eye view of the village, which looks no less charming now than it did by moonlight. The houses — chiefly with whitewashed walls, and roofs thatched or tiled — stand at all angles in an irregular circle round a hollow space of green. At this spot four or five roads converge, and the green is still further broken up by little paths in all directions. A stream runs through the bottom of the hollow. At the side where it passes into the meadows it is partly dammed up, which widens it to the dimensions of a pond; and over the dam runs a wooden foot-bridge. At the opposite side is a single-arched bridge of brick for heavier traffic, but the horses and cows seem to prefer going through the shallow water. All this we see from our open window, just outside of which hangs the sign of

Finchingfield — The Green Man. (now a private house).

Finchingfield — The Old Schoolhouse.

the *Green Man*, supported by some of the finest iron scroll-work to be seen anywhere — an achievement of some unnamed village blacksmith of old days.

Passing our parlour window, as we sit at breakfast, straggle the fresh-looking children on their way to school. Their way lies through the yard, and up two or three steps by a corner of the house, where there is a white gate leading into the churchyard. The church — thanks to a laudable and happily growing practice — stands always open. It represents all phases of Gothic. The oldest and stoutest portion of the structure is, of course, the tower, which has a good Norman doorway in its western front. With the lantern which surmounts it, it greatly resembles that of Felstead. Within the church is a monument to William Kemp, of Spain's Hall, who died in 1628, and was "master of himself so much, that what others scarce do by force and penalties, he did by a voluntary constancy hold his peace seven years." In such a man says a modern writer, it is impossible to feel any interest. Not so, surely, when we learn that he imposed this silence upon himself for some rash words in which he accused his wife of unfaithfulness.

On one side of the spacious burial-ground is the ancient almshouse, a long, low building with projecting upper storey; on the other is a deep hollow, whence stones and gravel were dug when the church tower was built. Beyond stretch the fields, bathed in the mellow light of early autumn

Even if you are not a sportsman or a dog, there is, at this season of the year, a peculiar satisfaction in rambling over the country, since you can go where you will across the stubble, if the lanes and innumerable footpaths do not content you. For that matter, in rural Essex, a quiet pedestrian can go practically anywhere. Notice-boards are almost non-existent. If you lose your way in somebody's fields, instead of being irascibly told that you are trespassing, you are courteously directed which way to go. It was on these terms that we explored the country round Finchingfield.

The character of the district is reflected in the names of its villages, most of which end in "field"; as Toppesfield, Great and Little Bardfield, Wethersfield. They are all more or less of the Finchingfield type, clustered round the church, embosomed in trees, and each intersected by its little river that finds its way along the narrow valleys, crossed here and there by a wooden bridge. One of these streams is still called the "Pant," an old Celtic word meaning "river."

Life moves very slowly in this remote part of Essex. The villagers still use the expression " going foreign " when they speak of visiting places but a few miles away. At Stambourne, some seven miles north of Finchingfield, Spurgeon noted a widespread belief in witchcraft in his boyhood ; and only a year or two ago I found this superstition still alive. Two fast-dying customs

— those of gleaning and the harvest-supper —
still flourish here ;   and the harvesters call the
gratuities they get from the sportsmen by the
Norman-French name of " largesse "   Nor do
the peasantry seem to have entirely relinquished
the old Catholic conception of life in favour of
Puritanism, if we may trust the experiences of
the Sunday we spent at Finchingfield.

Even the fields seemed to rest and rejoice in the
peaceful morning as we made our way over the
hill, to where, almost hidden among trees, stood
the church of Little Sampford, with its exquisitely-
proportioned Early English tower. The afternoon
was passed in a green arbour in the walled garden
of the inn. In the evening a harvest festival was
held. As we mounted the steps leading into the
churchyard, we saw the Norman doorway of the
tower standing open, and against a background of
light and flowers the figures of eight stalwart bell-
ringers in their shirt-sleeves forming a circle round
the font. Into the service which followed, the folk
entered with much heartiness; and the sincerity of
their thanksgiving was the less to be questioned, as
the harvest had been exceptionally good. Returning afterwards to the inn, we were surprised to
find it full to overflowing, with men, women and
children, all partaking of some refreshment on their
way homeward. There was plenty of talking and
animation, but no roughness or coarse language ;
and no one seemed to feel the least incongruity in

the change from one scene to the other. The prevailing impression was simply that of good-fellow-
ship. Well said the Psalmist :   " I see that all
things come to an end, but thy commandment is
exceeding broad."

XXVI

Inns and Churches

"Serve God and rejoice."

" *Servi Deo et gaude.*" These Latin words are to be found painted in black letters in the hollow moulding of the north or priests' doorway at Littlebury church near Saffron Walden ; and in a like position over the south or people's entrance appears the same exhortation in the vulgar tongue — " Serve God and rejoice. " When or by whom these words were placed there I cannot tell, but they seem to me to sum up the whole spirit of mediæval religion, and that is why I have set them at the head of this chapter.

Why in Essex as elsewhere do we nearly always find the village inn in close proximity to the village church ? The answer is simple enough. In the days when each village was practically self-contained, the church stood to the peasant for consolation in sickness and trouble, and for the celebration of the mysteries of his faith ; the inn for rest after labour, social intercourse, and re-creation. With all their essential differences of purpose, church and inn were alike in this, that they both ministered to the natural and universal needs of man.   Before the rise of Puritanism no incongruity between them was felt ;   rather they seemed to be necessary parts of one scheme of life.   It is perhaps only humerous exaggeration which prompts a modern poet to declare that

> " Malt does more than Milton can
> To justify God's ways to man ;"

but it was certainly a true instinct which led William Morris, in his " Dream of John Ball, " to describe his hero, when fettered in the Canterbury prison, as longing among other good things of the outer world, for " the talk of good fellows round the ale-house bench."

It may surprise some good people to hear that a house of call is not necessarily a haunt of vice. One may admire the zeal for humanity shown by temperance advocates and yet feel a doubt whether some of the sweeping changes they propose are applicable to all circumstances.   The notion that all licensed houses of entertainment are places where people are anxious to force strong drink upon you has been quite dispelled, so far as I am concerned, by a long experience of Essex inns ;   in which it has never seemed to make the slightest difference whether I took any intoxicant or not. In Essex, at all events, they have not forgotten what was declared in the preamble to an Act of Parliament so long ago as 1603 to be " the ancient true and principal use of inns . . . the receipt relief and lodging of wayfaring persons travelling from place to place. " Be it remembered that this office of hospitality was one of those formerly undertaken by the monasteries as a matter of course, and as a religious duty. Inns arose and flourished in England side by side with the monasteries ; and though the former must have increased in number and importance when the latter were swept away, the tradition of hospitable entertainment for travellers had taken firm root, and it has not yet died out. What an inestimable boon it is to a stranger, arriving in a village he has never seen before, to be able to go straight to the inn, with the moral certainty of receiving a friendly welcome, food, warmth, and rest!

In a village community, where the general level of education is low and opportunities for improvement rare, the inn is often both a school of manners and a centre of culture. In fairness it must be remembered that its doors are open to everybody, so that rough customers may occasionally be met there, and much depends on the personal character of the people who keep the house ; but it is strongly in the interest of the landlord to discourage not only drunkenness but coarse language and behaviour. The reader has already heard what was told to me at Pleshey, that neither drunkards nor teetotalers were known in the village. There is another little ale-house in the

Essex Weald, where the old couple who have kept it for a quarter of a century have never once had occasion to call in a policeman. In these inns the landlord is often a retired farmer or grazier, or carries on one of these occupations in conjunction with the inn, or perhaps some trade of especial service to travellers, such as that of wheelwright or smith. Quiet, law-abiding, God-fearing folk most of them are. Their wives and widows are like unto them, and of course it is the landlady on whom the traveller's comfort most depends. The mere fact that such people preside over the village inns goes far to prove my statement that the inn is a school of manners and a centre of culture. It is here that the neighbours come to hear and discuss the news of the day; and the most striking thing is the kindly and tolerant spirit which prevails, in contrast to many meetings held under, avowedly religious auspices. With all the gossip I have heard in inn parlours and kitchens, I can hardly recall the utterance of an uncharitable expression or the imputation of a mean motive to anyone. How universal the unwritten law of good-breeding is in Essex inns I had not consciously realised until one day I saw over a fireplace a frame containing these lines:

"Here stop and spend a social hour
In harmless mirth and fun :
Let friendship reign ; be just and kind,
And evil speak of none."

But while the inn has retained something of its primitive religious character, the church has almost wholly lost the mundane elements that once belonged to it. It is hard for us to think of these two great human institutions except as one purely secular and the other purely sacred. No such difficulty troubled our forefathers. These distinctions were hardly felt when daily life was penetrated with mystery, and the act of worship expressed what the whole of life implied. Looked at in this light, it is impossible to share the regret expressed by some clerical writers for the secular uses to which the church buildings were formerly put. These secular uses were very varied. The first and most obvious is of course that of defence and refuge in troublous times. This is illustrated in the earlier structures by the immense thickness of the walls and towers, the smallness of the apertures for doors and windows, and the splayed formation of the latter. The same idea seems to have been expressed in the battlements used as an ornamental feature at a later period when the need for them had passed away. Other secular uses continued much longer. " In pre-Reformation times, " says the Rev. J. E. Vaux in " Church Folklore, " "the naves of churches were places where tradesmen assembled for bargain and barter, where lawyers had interviews with their clients, where owners of property deposited their goods, and where divers courts of justice were held. . . . The naves of our cathedrals and parish churches seem to have been regarded as the common homes of the people. " The last remark I believe to be profoundly true. " From the Englishman's cradle, " says Mr Edward Smith, " the first thought of his parents was his baptism in the parish church, and the public churching of his mother. His approaching marriage was announced by banns being called in his parish church, as well as that of his bride. The ceremony was celebrated by the joyous pealing of the church bells. The church's festivals were his own holidays. The announcement of his death was conveyed to the parish and his neighbours by a solemn knell from the church tower. To be buried in the graveyard of his fathers was his last desire. Here collections for the poor were made, and public notices affixed to the doors. . . . The principal porch was the place of village assembly, and frequently the place of record for legal arrangements, judgements given, deeds signed. Over the porch the chamber was occupied by a school or by a library. The south porch was frequently used for housing vagrants ; indeed, every poor parishioner had the right to make it a shelter for the night in case of necessity. We have even records of women in childbirth being allowed to occupy the south porch. A hundred illustrations could be given of the relation of the church to the parish. But most important of all was that it stood the tangible source of moral instruction in every town and village. Seeing all this, how great is the value of these ancient buildings as historic monuments ! The intense interest felt in the architectural beauty of many of them simply pales before the sentiments aroused by a consideration of their human interest. The home of the national faith and morals for upwards of a thousand years — that is the parish church in England."

At St Mary's, Bocking, the expense of enlarging the church was defrayed by the profits of three mysteries, or miracle plays, acted in the nave. Another mode of procedure was followed at Thorpe-le-Soken, which the reader will remember as the scene of the romantic story of Kitty Canham ; where, on the beam of a screen, is the following inscription, in raised Gothic letters, on a scroll held by two angels : " This cost is the bachelors, made by ales theen he ther med. " Here we have an example of that curious mediæval custom, the Church Ale, of which Carew, in his " Survey of Cornwall, " has left so striking an account. " The neighbours met at the church-house, and there fed merrily on their own victuals, each contributing some petty portion to the stock, which by many smalls groweth to a meetly greatness ; for there is entertained a kind of emulation between the wardens, who by his graciousness in gathering, and good husbandry in expending, can best advance the church's profit. Besides, the neighbour parishes at those times lovingly visit one another, and in this way frankly spend their money together. The afternoons are consumed in such exercises as old and young folk (having leisure) do accustomly wear out the time withal. When the feast is ended, the wardens yield in their account to the parishioners, and such money as exceedeth the disbursements is laid up in store to defray any extraordinary charges arising in the parish or imposed on them for the good of the country, or the Prince's service, neither of which commonly gripe so much, but that somewhat still remaineth to cover the purse's bottom. " In the northern counties, according to Hutchins' " History of Northumberland," and doubtless elsewhere, these festivals were often held under tents and booths erected in the churchyard. Interludes were per-formed, "being a species of theatrical performance, consisting of some passage of Holy Scripture per-sonated by actors. " Aubrey, in his introduction to the " Natural History of Wiltshire, " says that there were no rates for the poor in his grand-father's days, the Church Ale at Whitsuntide doing the business. He describes how " in every parish was a church-house, to which belonged spits, crocks, and other utensils for dressing pro-visions. Here the housekeepers met. The young people were there too, and had dancing, bowling, shooting and butts, etc, the ancients sitting gravely by and looking on. All things were civil and with-out scandal. " But the Reformation changed all this. If we may believe Stubbs, the Church Ale had degenerated when he wrote his " Anatomie of Abuses " in 1585. " In this kind of practice they continued six weeks — a quarter of a year — yea, half a year together. That money, they say, is to repair their churches and chapels with, to buy books for service, cups for the celebration of the sacrament, and other such necessaries. " Stubbs shows that in his day feasts and entertainments were still held in churches, although this has been forbidden by a Canon of 1571 ; but the Church Ale must have died hard, for in 1683 it was necessary to enact in another Canon that " the churchwardens or questmen and their assistants shall suffer no plays, feasts, banquets, suppers, church-ale drinkings . . . in the church, chapel, or churchyard. " Only the faintest echo of those days of robust piety reaches us in this entry in the vestry minutes of Havering-atte-Bower. " At a vestry held at St Marie's Chappel, Havering, ye 9th of Nov. 1717. Agreed — Yt a pint of sack be allowed ye minister yt officiates ye Lord's Day ye winter season. "

Concerning the church-house, an eminent antiquary states that " not a single undoubted specimen has been spared to us ; though it is not improbable that the half timbered building attached to the west end of the church at Langdon, in Essex and now called the Priest House, is really one of these. " I am inclined to think that many an old house one sees at the edge of the churchyard may really have been the church-house. It is a pity that one cannot identify the buildings in which these Church Ales were held, at which " all things were civil and without scandal, " and which render the parallel between inns and churches so complete.

XXVII

The Soul of Essex

" Nothing is greater than simplicity."– *Whitman*

THE reader must have perceived that with me Essex is a passion — almost a religion. Sometimes in the London streets, especially during long sunny days, the thought comes over me of churches, inns, or clustered villages that I know, how they stand quietly through the hours, the sunlight travels round them and fades, and all the time perhaps there is no one there who appreciates their beauty as I do — at least I am not there. This thought brings a strange mixture of exaltation and despondency. When my desire is fulfilled, and I am bodily amidst the scenes I love, all else seems vain. I feel that I have come home ; and I ask myself, Why have I been away so long ? So much time seems to have been wasted. The curious thing is that there is no disillusion : everything seems more beautiful than I remembered or imagined it.

" Beautiful, nay solemn, was the sudden aspect to our wanderer, " says Carlyle, in a wonderful passage of " Sartor Resartus " " He gazed over those stupendous masses with wonder, almost with longing desire ; never till this hour had he known Nature, that she was one, that she was his mother, and divine. And as the ruddy glow was fading into clearness in the sky, and the sun had now departed, a murmur of eternity and immensity, of death and of life, stole through his soul; and he felt as if death and life were one, as if the earth were not dead, as if the spirit of the earth had its throne in that splendour, and his own spirit were therewith holding communion."

This also I have felt — as who has not ? Yet there is something else which needs to be expressed. Do not forests, mountains, the seashore, always leave one melancholy ? The human interest is wanting. Borrow's Petulengro was completely happy if he could only feel the wind on the heath ; but natural as this may be in the Ishmaels of humanity, the sober citizen craves for signs of a settled and ordered life. It is the bleeding of natural beauty with the human interest that wholly fills and satisfies us. This double need is met in different places in an infinite variety of ways; so that to the traveller every place he passes has a special character of its own. For, says Carlyle again, " always, of its own unity, the soul gives unity to whatsoever it looks on with love ; thus does the little dwelling-place of man, in itself a congeries of houses and huts, become for us an

Shenfield — The Hall.

Henham-on-the-Hill — Cottages.

individual, almost a person." Now the individuality of Essex has for me beyond that of all other places, a charm which I can hardly put into words.

In what does this consist ? It is characteristic of Essex that it has no cathedral. The presence of a magnificent mass of architecture such as that in a county seems to focus all the interest in it to that one point, and the country around it seems only its setting. In Essex the interest is more widely spread. It is not the great houses which attract me. The most beautiful of these date from the Tudor age ; but beautiful as they are, they represent an epoch which was fateful to its influence and hostile to what I conceive to be the real spirit of Essex. The models of them, often much of their materials. were brought from Italy along with Machiavellian statecraft and political centralisation. The great men of that epoch were many of them Essex men ; it was the favourite Court county, and these great houses were, and some of them still are, courts in little. Time has added a mellow charm to the few of them which remain, and they are wonderfully beautiful as buildings. Even so, not many of them have been left unspoilt. The imposing mansions of later date fail wholly to impress me. Buildings which merely represent the ideas of pride and exclusiveness have nothing intrinsically worshipful about them, the less when constructed in a

R

bald and tasteless style, or on a sham Greek or Renaissance model. Contrast any of them with the genuine architecture of the soil, in which everything has a use and a meaning, and note with what pleasure the eye rests upon the dignified and simple lines of an old church, farmhouse or inn.

Of picturesqueness, that indefinable yet very definite quality, I find this clear scientific explanation by Dr Alfred Russel Wallace : " Why are the old cottages so invariably picturesque, so harmonious with the surrounding landscape in form and colour as to be a constant delight to the artist and lover of Nature ? The answer, I believe, is, because they were the natural product of the time and locality, being built by the very people who were to live in them, with materials found in the district, and in the style which experience had shown to be at once the most convenient and the most economical. The first owners of these old cottages, the men who built them, were either freeholders or copyholders, or those who had obtained land on lease for several lives, and they were actually erected in part by the men themselves, with the assistance of their neighbours, the village carpenter and mason. The materials were obtained either from their own land or from the moors, wastes, and woodlands, which were then open for the use of all the inhabitants of the manor. The walls were

of rough stone or of brick, or timber-framed
with rough-hewn wood in the upper storey,
forming those charming wood-framed houses of
Surrey, Sussex, Hereford, and some other
counties.   In Dorset and Devon the walls were
often of clay mixed with straw, called ' cobble, '
and this makes a far warmer, drier, and altogether more desirable dwelling than the modern
brick, as many of the old cottages, which have
lasted for centuries, prove.   The roof, framed
with rough posts, and with poles for rafters,
has a slight irregularity of outline very pleasing
to the eye when compared to the rigid straightness, flatness, and angularity of roofs built with
machine-cut timber ;   while the thick covering of
thatch, broken by the small rounded dormer
windows and with the broadly-overhanging eaves,
is not only far warmer in winter and cooler in
summer than any tiled or slated roof, but has
the inestimable advantage to the labourer that he
can repair it himself. "

It will be observed that this attempt to account
for the picturesqueness of our old villages pre-
supposes an earlier and simpler state of society —
in a word, the village community, which recent
research has shown to have been the root of
Aryan civilisation, as it is still to some extent
the basis of English country life.   Now it is just
this which is suggested by the outward aspect
of the village, with its houses clustered into a

single street or grouped around a common green
The main features of the village community —
with whatever modifications you please — are still
to be traced.   There is first the dependence of
the village upon the land.   This is still an actual
fact — and the very look of a village surrounded by
its fields and pastures proclaims it.   Alas ! but
little is left of the admirable old system under
which each household in a manor had a share
in everything necessary for the maintenance of
a simple life — woodland, arable, pasture, and
meadow.   Students have been puzzled by the
complexity of the arrangement by which the
holding of each proprietor was scattered in small
strips over various parts of the manor, subject to
frequent redistribution ;   but this seems to have
been devised for the very purpose of securing to
each a fair share of everything, good or bad.
Faint traces of this system still survive.   " In the
Stour valley, " says Mr C. J. Cornish, " with
Essex on one side and Suffolk on the other, are
numbers of common meadows in which several
men own portions, which they agree to feed or
mow, as they may decide, every year. "   The
second feature of the village community, closely
related to the first, is that each village was
practically self-contained.   Each had its own
smith, its own carpenter, its own constable, and
so on, while the main business, that of agri-
aculture was largely carried on in common.   Even

the church was the church of the community, and the priest was the priest of the people. It followed from this, again, that while the village was largely independent of what went on outside its borders, inter-dependence was the rule within. Town-bred people to-day are astonished at the freedom with which rustic folk enter into each other's houses, and at the minuteness with which they discuss their neighbours' affairs. I verily believe that " village gossip " is largely a survival from an earlier time ; this interest in each other's business seems to them even now quite natural and proper, and is by no means regarded as ill-natured curiosity. Centralisation, travel, all that we call progress, tends to destroy all these linger-ing traces of the communal mode of life ; but I confess that I regard their disappearance with dismay, and I can hardly conceive of a more admirable state of society than the village com-munity at its best.

To what do we owe the relics that have come down to us of this primitive system and all that it implies ? Not to the Romans, who came here as conquerors, and notwithstanding the prac-tical arts they introduced, were after all but splen-did aliens. Not to the Northmen, who came as plunderers, " the locusts of the North, " as an old chronicler graphically calls them. Denizens of a barren country, and accustomed to live by pillage, it was long before they could bring themselves to settle under a peaceable and orderly government. Not to the Normans, who had all the instincts of the Northmen from whose blood they sprang, tinctured with the civilisation of Gaul. It is surely to the Saxons that we owe the village community as it has come down to us. Fierce and quarrelsome, they were yet essentially cultivators. We have seen how the rich lands of Essex attracted them, and how they came here, not for dominion or for booty, but to settle and thrive. They found no use for the walled towns of Roman Britain which lay ready to their hand, but built their timber homesteads amid the broad acres. It is they who have stamped their virile language upon the placenames of the county, just as it is their speech that is still spoken and their customs that still survive.

The fact that under the feudal system the peasant was bound to the soil has been treated as evidence that the village community is a development of the Roman villa owned by a lord and cultivated by slaves. In this way it has even been sought to account for the striking fact that the tenant's holding passed from father to son as a matter of right. These things seem to me to point less to servitude than to freedom. Our forefathers had hardly any conception of a man without the means of life, and the possession of a definite right to the use of land in the place of his birth was what constituted him a freeman. How did this idea evolve into the serfdom of the Middle Ages?

Every Essex village has its " hall, " or manor-house ; several of them have two or three. Some descriptive writers have mourned over the fact that many of these manor-houses have " degenerated " into mere farms. If I am not mistaken, this is simply a reversion to their original use. The manor-houses built in Tudor and even earlier times were often merely the country-houses of wealthy and distinguished families ; but that the manor-house was at first simply the principal farmstead in the village community I have no doubt. The " lord " of the manor had his strips of land with the rest of his neighbours, and the work he could demand of them was strictly limited by custom. Just as in later times his power and influence increased until he at length became the only person of consequence in the place, so it is probable that at an earlier stage he was simply the head man of the village. If he enjoyed especial priveleges, he was still identified with the common interest, and between him and his neighbours there was a bond of reciprocal service. Leadership in battle, and the office of magistrate, allied functions in a rude state of society, were probably the chief forms in which the service of the lord was rendered. I suppose the hall was originally the chief home-stead, where the lord lived surrounded by his clan in the old patriarchal fashion. That the relation between him and his followers may in Saxon times have been of a close and even affectionate character is abundantly clear from the allusions to Brihtnoth in the precious fragment of the *Song of Maldon*. Traces of the same spirit are found even under the Norman régime. From a study of the manorial records of Borley, near the northern boundary of Essex, relating to the thirteenth century , a learned foreign writer is led to observe :   " Very common is the practice of providing a meal for the labourers on the *boon-days*, the days on which the whole population of the village had to work for the lord in the most busy time of the summer and autumn. Such boon-work was considered as a kind of surplus demand ; it exceeded the normal distribution of work. It is often mentioned accordingly that such service is performed out of affection for the lord, and sometimes it gets the eloquent name of *love-bene.* "   It is curious to note that in the Stour valley the chief harvester is called " the lord. "   Is this merely rustic humour, or does it date from the remote time when the lord was simply the leading man in all village affairs ? It is undoubtedly an old term. Miss Betham-Edwards had recently published a story called " The Lord of the Harvest, " which illustrates this custom. And in the life of Constable it is recorded how a rustic friend of his, one Strowger, came up to London and had a private view of some of that artist's pictures then about to be exhibited. " He was captivated by one of them, a *Corn-field with reapers at work*, and pointed out to the arranging committee its correctness, the *lord* being in due advance of the rest." Readers of *Anna Karenina* will remember the wonderful chapter — surely a piece of autobiography — in which Tolstoy describes the experiences of a nobleman who spent a day mowing a field with his peasants ; and they may think that my interpretation of this quaint expression is not too far fetched.

" The influence of traditional ideas, " says Mr Gomme, " and of habits and ways that have come down to us from that far-off time which memory and fancy hold so dear, transcends and keeps in check even the forces of political economy which we have been taught to look upon as so irresistable ; and it is worth bearing in mind that some of the features of the village community are not very far removed from the socialism of to-day. In the history of human thought it will be found that the influences of traditional ideas far outweigh the influences of philosophy. "

The influences derived from tradition are happily still strong in Essex. Thus it happens that we are not left in the melancholy task of disinterring dead customs and ideas, or of cherishing vague regrets for a vanished past. Here, in the actual present, at our very doors, there is a beauty, a charm, a romance, which must be experienced to be understood, and which in these pages I have only been able to hint at. How shall I describe it ? The friendly simplicity of the landscape, of the homes of the people, and of the people themselves — this is the soul of Essex.

TOPOGRAPHICAL INDEX

PRINTED BY THE LAVENHAM PRESS LTD